Munch

MUNCH AND PHOTOGRAPHY

supported by
NORTHERN
ARTS

Contents

ISBN 0947940200

Foreword

This year, 1989, is the 150th anniversary of the invention of photography which makes it singularly appropriate that the remarkable exhibition, *'Munch and Photography'* should take place in Newcastle. Munch's photographs, as this extraordinary collection reveals, were at first haphazard and then later, purposeful and they played a seminal part in the creation of some of his most important paintings. Here, then, we have an opportunity of seeing the great Norwegian master's mind at work, just as intimately as if we had examined his sketch-books. We can note, for instance, how photographic effects such as double-exposure were translated almost directly into painterly inventions.

This exhibition, however, is in fact the fourth important Munch collection to have been organised by the Newcastle Polytechnic Gallery during the last decade, an indication not only of the valuable rapport which has been established with the Munch Museum in Oslo, to whom we are immensely grateful, but of the broader friendly ties between the region and Norway. It is, too, a further demonstration of that resourcefulness recommended in Kipling's poem, '*The Glory of the Garden*', wherein he declares that:

"Our England is a garden, and such gardens are not made
By singing: 'Oh, how beautiful!' and sitting in the shade
While better men than we go out and start their working lives
At grubbing weeds from gravel paths with broken dinner-
knives".

As this would suggest, the funding for the exhibition has in large part come from private companies: indeed without their help it is doubtful if it would have taken place at all. These companies broadly divide into those which are based within the Tyne and Wear area and those which are British branches of Norwegian parent companies. I realise that sponsorship of the visual arts is not always perceived as the most advantageous form of patronage, save when the exhibition has some guaranteed touristic aspect. I have been all the more delighted therefore, with the ready enthusiasm with which these companies have responded to our request for support of this highly serious exhibition. We greatly appreciate their help. In particular I must acknowledge the invaluable contribution made by:

Fred Olsen Lines; Scansped; Northern Arts; Norsk Hydro (UK) Rubb Buildings Limited; Kavli Limited; NEK Cables Limited; Seabay Limited; Phillips Petroleum Company (UK) Limited; P C B Bruce; The National Westminster Bank, Glaxochem Limited; Nycomed (UK) Limited; IBM Limited and the Museums and Galleries Commission.

A further pleasure resides in the fact that the exhibition is in fact being presented at the Hatton Gallery of Newcastle University. This is not so unusual insofar as the exhibition of paintings by Frans Widerberg, one of Norway's most celebrated contemporary artists, though organised by the Polytechnic Gallery, actually took place at the Hatton in 1987, an early example of a collaboration which we hope will yield many further possibilities. In this respect, the moral (and financial) support given to this project by the University Vice-Chancellor, Professor Laurence Martin; the Director of the Hatton Gallery, Dr John Milner and the Director of Exhibitions, William Varley, has been extremely welcome.

Norway's representatives in Newcastle, the Hon Nigel Westwood, Consul and Mrs McNamara, Vice-Consul, have been no less supportive in their heartening encouragement of our efforts to develop our links with Norway.

However, the unique association the Polytechnic Gallery has with the Munch Museum, exists today entirely due to the goodwill, dedication and willingness of the latter's staff to promote a greater understanding of Munch's oeuvre internationally. To this extent we, in the North East of England, have benefitted significantly. I wish, therefore, to thank Alf Bøe, Director; Arne Eggum, Chief Curator; Gerd Woll, Curator; Jan Thurman-Møe, Chief Restorer and Ingebjörg Gunnarson, Administrator, for their time, encouragement, fortitude, friendship and patience throughout our negotiations.

My ad hoc team have worked hard to make the exhibition come to fruition. They are: Sarah, Suzanne and Andrew, general administration; Stephanie Batty, my assistant and Stephen and Susan Bland, our gifted designers of the catalogue and supporting publicity material. They, too, deserve the warmest praise for their contribution.

Finally, I would like to gratefully acknowledge the invaluable support and confidence in our endeavours by Professor Tom Bromly, Dean of the Faculty of Art and Design. Without his, and the Polytechnic's, endorsement of this initiative, it would not have been possible to present this exhibition by Edvard Munch, one of the 20th century's indisputable masters.

Mara-Helen Wood
Curator
Newcastle Polytechnic Gallery.

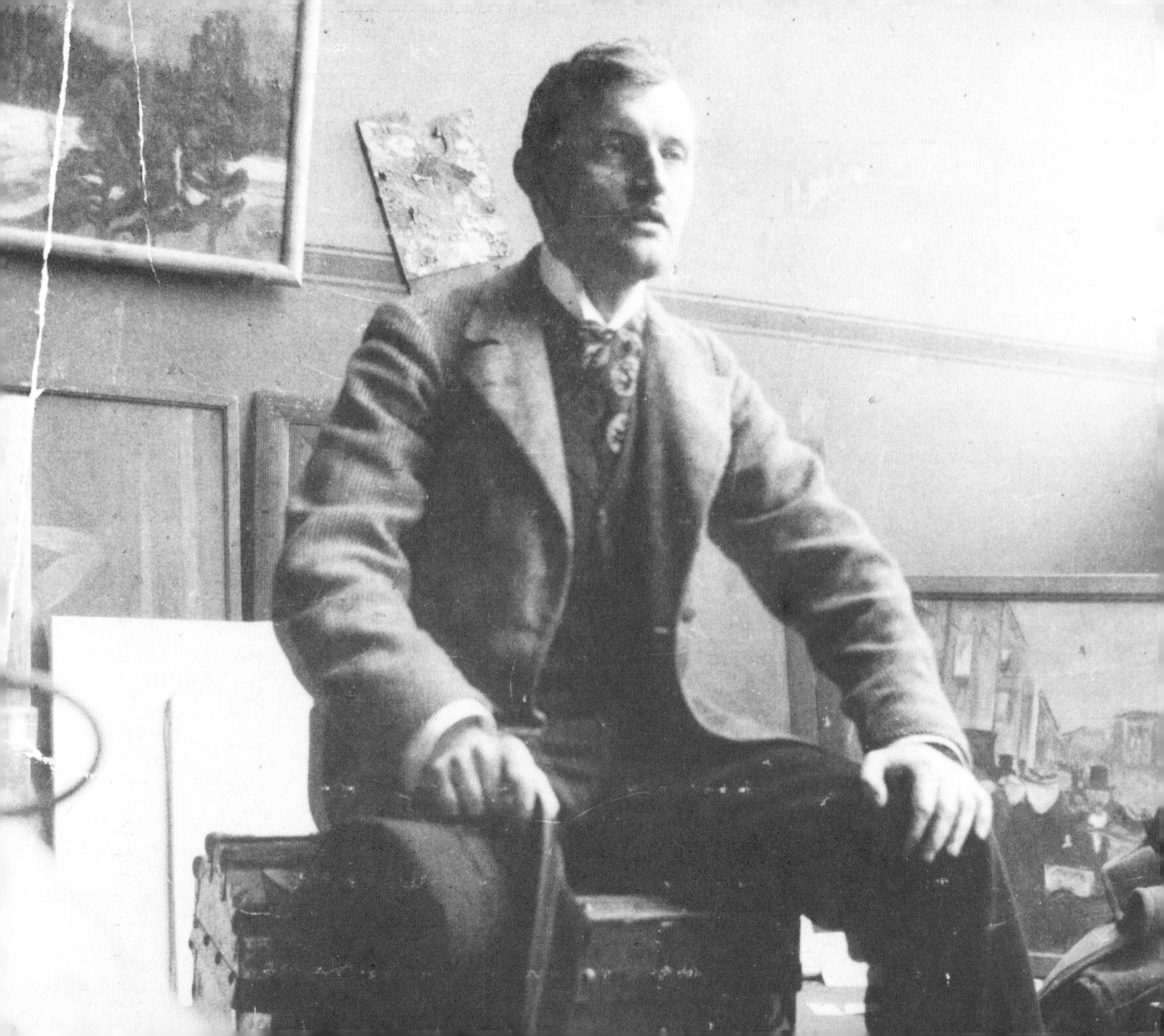

Biography

1863 12th December. Edvard Munch born to Dr Christian Munch and Laura Cathrine, nee Bjølstad, at Løten in Norway.

1864-68 The Family moves to Christiania (now Oslo). Munch's - mother dies of tuberculosis at the age of 33 and her sister Karen Bjølstad takes over as housekeeper.

1877 Munch's sister Sophie dies of tuberculosis at the age of 15.

1879-80 Enters Technical College to study architecture but leaves a year later to study art history and to become a painter.

1881 August. Enters the School of Drawing.

1882 Rents a studio with six other artists, with Christian Krohg as tutor.

1883 Participates in his first group exhibitions in Oslo, 'Art and Industry'and the 'Autumn Exhibition'. Visits Fritz Thaulow's 'open air studio'at Modum.

1884 Associates with the Christiania-Boheme, avant-garde painters and writers who meet at the Grande Cafe.

1885 May. Travels via Antwerp (The World Exhibition) to Paris. Begins painting *'The Sick Child'*, *'Puberty'*, and *'The Morning After'* which are completed a year later.

1886 Exhibits four paintings at the Autumn Exhibition in Oslo. '*The Sick Child*' provokes violent objections particularly from the Naturalistic painters.

1889 First one-man show in April. Granted a State Scholarship in July. Rents a house in Åsgårdstrand during the summer. Spends autumn in Paris where he attends Léon Bonnat's studio. Writes the 'St Cloud Manifesto'. Father dies in November.

1890 Returns to Norway in May. Summer in Åsgårdstrand. Returns to France in November. Receives his second State Scholarship and returns to France in November.

1891 Granted his third State Scholarship. Summer spent in Norway. Travels via Copenhagen to Paris in the Autumn and Nice in December. Exhibitions in Oslo, Berlin and Munich.

1892 Nice, Oslo and Åsgårdstrand. Meets Willumsen at his exhibition in Oslo. Munch's exhibition at the Verein Berliner Künstler (Association of Berlin Artists) in November, closes after one week.

1893 Berlin. Moves in literary circles and meets Richard Dehmel, Julius Meier-Graefe, August Strindberg, Dagny Juel, Stanislaw Przybyszewski and the editors of the magazine 'Pan'. Travels around Germany with the show which closed in Berlin in '92. The '*Frieze of Life*' begins to take shape.

1894 Berlin. Produces his first etchings and lithographs. The first book about Munch is published in July. September in Stockholm. Winter in Berlin.

1895 Paris in June. Exhibits at the 'Salon des Indépendants' and at the 'Salon de l'Art Nouveau'. The Meier-Graefe portfolio with eight etchings is published. Munch's brother Andreas dies.

1896 From Berlin to Paris. Exhibits 10 paintings at the 'Salon des Indépendants'. Works on illustrations for Baudelaire's 'Les Fleurs du Mal'. Contact with the Symbolists connected with Mallarmé. Produces designs for Ibsen's 'Peer Gynt' and 'John Gabriel Borkman' at the Théâtre de l'Oeuvre, Paris. Meets Delius. Prints colour lithographs and produces his first woodcut.

1897 Many exhibitions. Travel to Paris, Stockholm, Brussels, St Petersburg, Berlin.

1898 Norway, Copenhagen, Berlin, Paris. Illustrations to Munch/Strindberg's issue of the periodical 'Quickborn'. Meets Tulla Larsen.

1899 Berlin, Paris, Nice, Florence and Rome to study Raphael. Munch commits himself to a sanatorium in Kornhaug. Sister Laura institutionalised for schizophrenia.

1900 Munch leaves the Kornhaug sanatorium. To Berlin then to another sanatorium in Switzerland. Back to Norway in the autumn.

1901 Summer in Åsgårdstrand. Winter in Berlin. Dagny Juel murdered in Russia.

1902 Winter, Spring in Berlin. Albert Kollman introduces Munch to Dr Max Linde of Lübeck who writes a book on Munch and commissions him to produce a portfolio of 14 etchings and 2 lithographs. The relationship with Tulla Larsen ends in violence and Munch loses a finger joint on his left hand. Introduced to Gustav Schiefler, who begins to catalogue all the graphic works. Exhibits 22 paintings from the '*Frieze of Life*' in Berlin.

1903 Berlin and Paris. Joins the 'Société des Artistes Indépendants'. Meets Eva Mudocci. Depicts her in three lithographs, *'Madonna: The Brooch'*, *'Salome'* and *'The Violin Concert'*. Visits Dr Linde in Lübeck, paints his four sons and a frieze for his home.

1904 Berlin. Contract with Bruno Cassirer for exclusive rights to the sale of prints in Germany and a contract with Commeter in Hamburg for the sale rights of his paintings. Exhibits 20 paintings at the Vienna Secession. Linde Frieze rejected. Meets Elizabeth Förster-Nietzsche, sister of the philospher.

1905 Berlin. Exhibition in Prague (121 works). Herman Esswein writes a book on Munch. Bad Elgersburg, Thüringen in November to convalesce.

1906 Germany. Meets Swedish banker and patron Ernst Thiel for for whom he paints Nietzsche from a photograph. Designs stage sets for Ibsen's 'Ghosts' and 'Hedda Gabler' for Max Reinhardt's theatre in Berlin. Paints '*Self-Portrait with Bottle of Wine'*.

1907 Winter in Berlin. Produces designs for the foyer of Reinhardt's theatre. April in Stockholm. Summer and autumn in Warnemünde.

1908 Berlin. Paris. Spring and Summer in Warnemünde. Begins to paint scenes of workers and industry. Autumn, suffers a breakdown and is admitted to Dr Daniel Jacobson's clinic in Copenhagen. Is made a Knight of the Royal Order of St Olav.

1909 Winter and Spring in Copenhagen at the clinic. Produces '*Alpha and Omega*' series of lithographs based on his prose poetry and series of animal studies. May in Norway at Kragerø. Exhibition in June in Bergen of 100 paintings, 200 prints. Starts Work on the murals for the Oslo University Hall (Aula)

1910 Buys the Ramme estate at Hvitsten on the Oslo Fjord.

1911 August. Aula competition. Starts modelling in clay.

1912 Is given *place of honour* at the Sonderbund exhibition in Cologne. Meets Curt Glaser, print connoisseur and art historian. Six paintings shown in New York.

1913 Berlin. At the Autumn exhibition Munch and Picasso, the only foreigners invited to exhibit, given their own rooms. Rents Grimsröd Manor. Munch's 50th birthday.

1914 Winter, Paris and Berlin. Summer at Kragerø, Hvitsten and at Jeløya. 29th May University finally accepts his murals for the Aula. Paints '*Workers Returning Home*'.

1915 Hvitsten.

1916 January. Buys an estate at Ekely, near Oslo where he spends most of his time up to his death. Aula murals unveiled on 19th September.

1917 Curt Glaser's book on Munch is published.

1918 Ekely. Publishes pamphlet on '*The Frieze of Life*'.

1919 Catches 'Spanish Flu'. November - December exhibits 57 prints in New York.

1920-21 Berlin. Paris. Wiesbaden. Frankfurt.

1922 Paints frieze for the Freia Chocolate Factory. April, Berlin. Supports German artists by buying 73 prints. May, Zürich.

1923 Becomes a member of the German Academy.

1924 Summer, Bergen. Supports German artists again.

1925 Elected honorary member of the Bavarian Academy of Visual Arts, Munich.

1926 Sister Laura dies. Spring. Lübeck, Berlin, Venice, Munich and Wiesbaden. October, Copenhagen, Berlin, Paris.

1927 Second volume of Schiefler's catalogue of Munch's graphic works published. Major retrospective exhibitions in Berlin and at the National Gallery, Oslo.

1928 Works on designs for the Oslo City Hall. 5 Paintings exhibited in San Francisco.

1929 Builds outdoor 'winter studio' at Ekely.

1930 Blood-vessel ruptures in Munch's right eye and causes almost total blindness.

1931 Munch's aunt Karen Bjölstad dies.

1933 Made a Knight of the Order of the Grand Cross of St Olav. Jen Thiis and Pola Gauguin's first biographies published in Norway. Munch's 70th birthday.

1936 Exhibits in Britain for the first time, at the Scottish Academy in Edinburgh.

1937 Eighty-two works by Munch in public collections in Germany confiscated and considered 'degenerate' by the Nazis.

1938 Eye trouble returns.

1939 January 23. Auction in Oslo of 57 prints from German Museums.

1940 German occupation of Norway. Paints between '*Clock and Bed*'.

1942 34 prints exhibited in Brooklyn Museum.

1943 Munch's 80th Birthday. Produced his last print, a lithograph of Hans Jaeger. Windows of the house blown out by a Nazi bomb. Munch catches cold and becomes ill.

1944 23 January. Ekely. Munch dies peacefully. Bequeaths his estate to the City of Oslo. Approximately 1,000 paintings, 15,400 prints, 4,500 watercolours and drawings and six sculptures. Also 155 copper plates, 143 lithographic stones, 133 woodblocks and a library of almost 6,000 items.

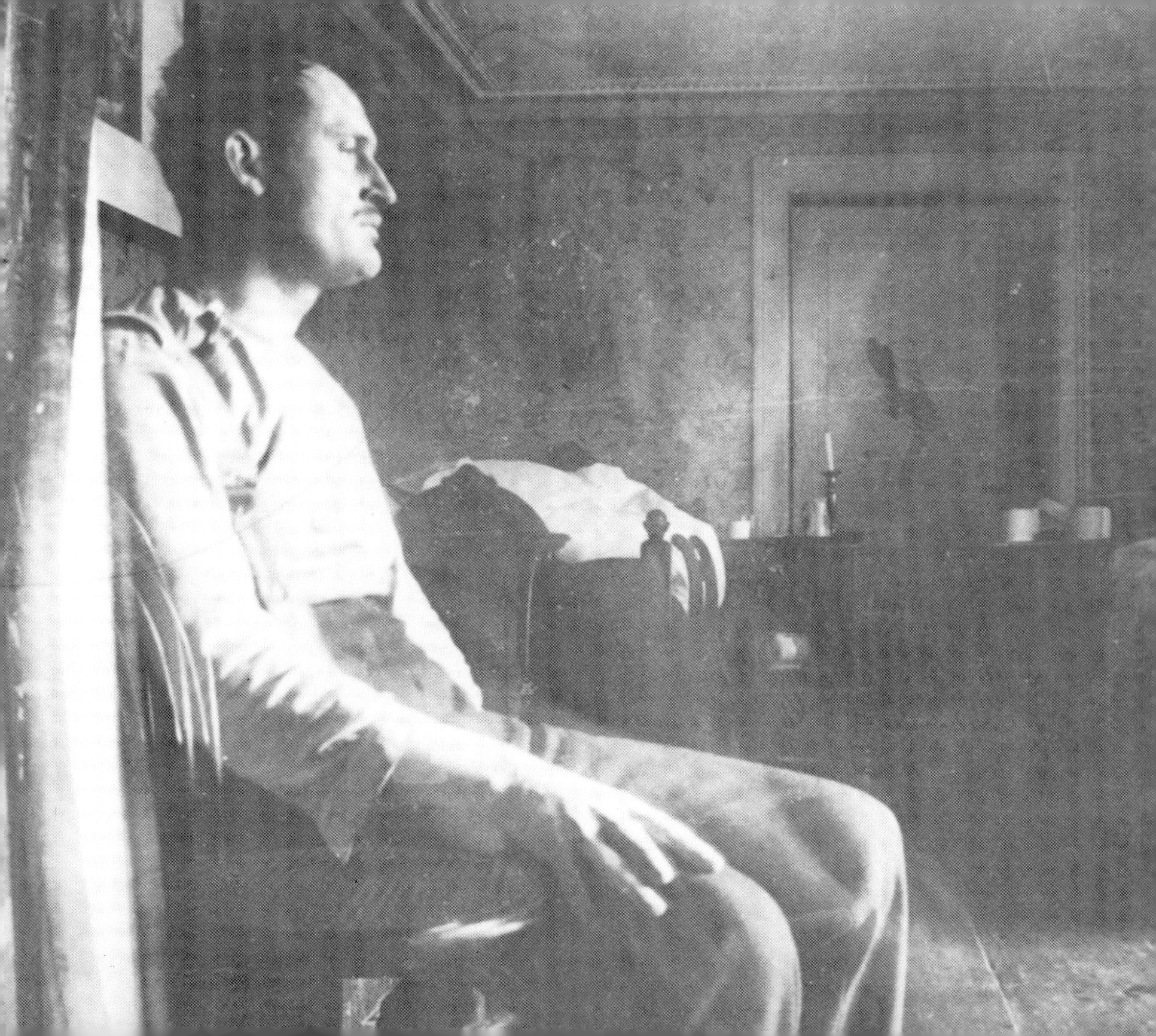

Edvard Munch - his life and art

Edvard Munch wrote in the so-called St. Cloud Manifesto, probably at the turn of the year 1889: ...*"One ought no longer to paint interiors with people sitting reading and women knitting. The subject should be living human beings who are breathing and feeling, suffering and loving."* He thus created a purpose for his art: to put the human being's experience of life at the centre of his oeuvre.

The chief problem behind the development of a series of his most important subjects at that time was the human problem of identity in man's relationship with society, with nature and with the essential self; and like Dostoevsky, Sören Kierkegaard and Sigmund Freud, he took advantage of his unique psychological insights.

No other artist developed such a peculiarly personal symbolism originating in his own traumatic experience as Munch. He *crystallized* these feelings into the pictorial expression of man's deepest emotional experiences: the zenith of art.

The existential way of exposing his inner life foreshadowed something new in pictorial art. Such an expressionism in Munch's sense is an extremely subjective art with something unsophisticated and primitive intact. One of his friends from Berlin wrote of this in the 1890's: *"He does not need to go to Tahiti to see and experience the primitive in human nature. He carries his own Tahiti inside...."*

Man's subjectivity has parallels in both Henrik Ibsen's and August Strindberg's writing. Like their art, it builds on Sören Kierkegaard's hypothesis that truth is intimacy; it is only through subjective engagement that one can attain insight into human experience.

Like Kierkegaard's philosophy, Munch's art is a direct forerunner of the philosophical existentialism which flourished in the years after the Second World War, as we clearly find in Albert Camus and Jean-Paul Sartre.

In that way it seems inevitable that Munch saw his paintings as a link in the tradition of the creation of pictorial art by Michelangelo, Grünewald,

Rembrandt, Van Gogh and Gauguin, all artists who reflected and searched profoundly in the human psyche in their art.

Edvard Munch was born at Løten in Hedmark on 12 December 1863. The family rented rooms from a farm near a military establishment where his father was the medical officer with the rank of lieutenant. On his father's side Munch belonged to an old Norwegian family, with many intellectually and artistically gifted members. P A Munch, a leading Norwegian historian, was his uncle; the painter Edvard Diriks was his cousin. But Munch grew up in an isolated and quite modest professional home. The family moved to Kristiania (later known as Oslo) when Edvard was a year old. For many years the family lived at Grünerløkka, one of Kristiania's working-class areas. Here his father, rather unsuccessfully, tried to establish a practice as a doctor, as well as his position as medical officer, promoted now to the rank of captain. His mother came from a more practical family of sea captains characterised by vigour to a greater degree than the intellectual virtues. His father's melancholy temperament, his own poor health, and his mother's and sister Sophie's illnesses and deaths, darkened Munch's formative years. In his art he constantly turned back to these unhappy memories. When his mother died in 1868, her younger sister, Karen Bjølstad, took over the housekeeping. This strong and unselfish woman became for many years the focus of the little family.

After having attended the Technical School with the intention of becoming an architect, Munch made up his mind in 1880 to become a painter. He became a student at the School of Drawing from 1881. In the autumn of 1882 he rented a studio at the *Pultosten* (The Soft Cheese) in Parliament Square in the centre of Kristiania, where Kristian Krohg, a leading Norwegian painter at the time, taught a group of young painters.

At this time there was great turmoil in artistic circles in Kristiania. New ideas from Paris were breaking the old academic traditions. It was felt that one was living in a time of conflict and transition: that the foundation of art would have to be built anew. Munch took this as a personal challenge. He experimented throughout his whole life to concentrate the essence of life in his art.

Munch's work from this time was particularly characterized by a large group of portrait studies which began to reveal a distinct ability for sure characterization. The young artists at *Pultosten* preferred to bring in models from the street: old men and women, marked by life. The artists also modelled for each other. Beside Christian Krohg with his background of the most advanced German painting, Fritz Thaulow, with his French-inspired naturalism, became Munch's chief rôle model. The first pictures Munch exhibited clearly show the influence of these two artists, but they also show evidence of a developing individual character.

Before Munch was twenty years old he took part for the first time in an exhibition at the Industry and Art Exhibition in Kristiania in 1883, where he was represented by a portrait painting. Munch was soon regarded as undoubtedly the most gifted among the young artists, but also the most extreme regarding style and artistic development. The judgement that Munch's art revealed ability, but that he lacked the will to finish his work, continued for more than a year in the radical press, which was otherwise supportive of his art. In the controversial press Munch was seen as one-sided, and condemned as a socialist, even as an anarchist.

A trip to the World Exhibition in Antwerp in 1885, and then a visit to Paris, brought Munch into contact with the latest movements in European art. His brush strokes became freer and broader and he fused - in a way seen by his contemporaries as impudent - both impressionistic and naturalistic elements. Most striking is his full-figure portrait of his friend Jensen-Hjell, where, to the irritation of the critics, only the reflection on the lorgnette was depicted, not the eye itself. The portrait reflected the whole international tradition of portraiture since Velasquez, and indicates that Munch had seen Edouard Manet's portraits in Paris. The picture was interpreted as an example of artistic delusion: impressionism. But at the same time Munch demonstrated an ambition to exceed naturalistic realism and to express strong individual feelings. He painted his first versions of ***Puberty*** and ***The Morning After The Night Before*** which have both been lost. But the most striking example of these new endeavours is his first creation: ***The Sick Child*** from 1885-86, now in the National Gallery in Oslo. A concentrated style and a highly personal technique interpreted the artist's experience of the death of his sister eight years earlier.

Portrayal of sick-beds was very common at the time, when naturalism was the dominant mode of art, but Munch explained his particular solution thus: *"I maintain that there was not one of these painters who lived in such a way through the last agonising drink of their subject as I did in* ***The Sick Child****. For it was not only I who sat there - it was all my dear ones."*

The Sick Child (the version from 1921 - 22) shows perhaps first and foremost Munch's ability for psychological insight into a young person's resigned farewell to an unlived life. In its original development, ***The Sick Child*** was still more clearly influenced by technical experiments than the picture appears today. Munch made it not only an unconventional expression of his feelings, but scratched lines in the impasted paint with a knife or palette knife. Originally he also let thin paint run down the canvas in fine stripes, as if he saw the subject through running tears or trembling eyelashes. These stripes later disappeared when the picture was painted-over in the 1890's. As expressive and innovative as this work of art is, one cannot imagine it being created without the artist having formulated, at least to himself, the rudiments of an existential expressionistic aesthetic.

Both the development of the subject itself and the misty, quite unreal, atmosphere which surrounded the deceased (his mother and his sister Sophie) had a compelling similarity to the *Spirit Photography* typical of the time. A lively debate took place in Kristiania about spiritualistic phenomena just as Munch was working on this painting, which can at least partly explain the picture's expression of a *spiritual shell*, as Jens Thiis describes it. However, the painting made a shocking impact when it was exhibited at the Autumn Exhibition of 1886, unique in Norwegian art history. It actually unleashed a storm of indignation and protest.

The main tendency in Munch's art at the end of the 1880s was, however, a realistic art, as one sees in the bravura-piece ***Spring*** (probably meant for the Salon or World Exhibition in Paris) and the psychological portrait of the writer and Bohemian Hans Jaeger, both from 1889.

Although posterity has seen something of a development towards a more traditional style in Munch's art from this period, he was regarded by the critics and fellow students to an ever-increasing extent as being the incarnation of radical art. This may be due partly to Munch retaining his freedom of expression while the other Norwegian artists at that time worked towards a drier, more photographic realism.

In 1889 Munch was given a State Scholarship which gave him the opportunity to spend the next three winters studying in France. Most of the paintings from that period are influenced by impressionism and stem directly from the influence of Monet, Pissarro and Seurat.

Munch realised, however, that the impressionistic imperative to produce transient effects is, in principle, impossible. Impressionism becomes in the final analysis a knack of memory. As Munch himself expressed it: *"I don't paint what I see, but what I saw."* Gradually there began to appear a stronger emotional content in his work, particularly in some of his landscapes and figure compositions, inspired by the coastline of the little fishing village of Åsgårdstrand, where he spent his summers.

In 1892 Munch was invited to exhibit in the Verein Berliner Künstler, where his pictures aroused a scandal to such a degree that the exhibition had to be closed. Munch immediately became the talk of the town, and social circles in Berlin immediately opened their doors, but not their purses, to him. The doors were thus opened to him in the radical literary milieu around

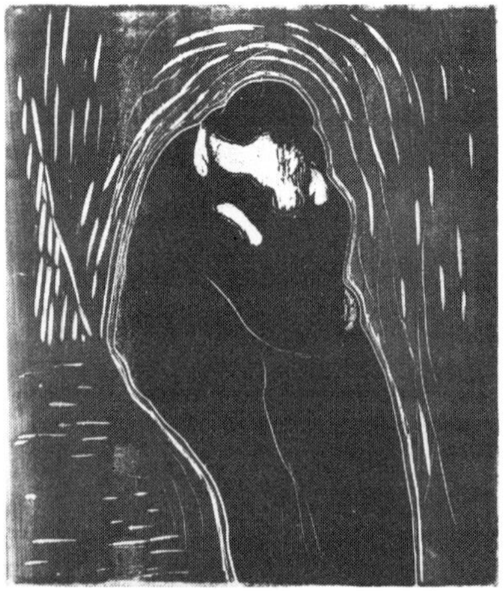

The Kiss, 1897-98 Colour woodcut

August Strindberg who held court at the *Black Piglet Bar* (*Zum Schwarzen Ferkel*). This circle included among others the Polish writer Stanislaw Przybyszewski, the German art historian Julius Meier-Graefe and the young experimental writer Richard Dehmel. Here he painted, among other pictures, the bluish portrait of Dagny Juel, Przybyszewski's young Norwegian wife. She is standing full face with her arms behind her back, surrounded by a shining aureola, smiling towards the onlooker with half-closed eyes. Strindberg, who saw the painting being created in Munch's studio, described it to his fiancée as being *"a spiritual rather than a physical seduction."*

The so-called Ferkel-circle with its interest in symbolism and Nietzsche's philosophy, with its preoccupation with erotic problems and death fantasies, reinforced the most basic aspects of Munch's psyche and the idea of the ***Frieze of Life*** developed. He imagined it as a series of pictures with the theme taken from the spiritual life of man, related above all to love and death. ***The Kiss***, ***The Scream***, ***The Vampire***, ***Madonna***, ***Melancholy***, ***Jealousy*** and ***Death in the Sick Room*** all express a strongly pessimistic attitude and are painted in a concentrated *expressionistic* style, where colour is used more symbolically and musically than descriptively. He wanted to depict and articulate his own experiences of emotional feeling for the subject - the spiritual - not nature herself. He used a repertoire of pictorial and architectonic effects, and a whole set of keys and symbols, like the reflection of the moon over water in the form of a column, or a set shadow which could join a group of people or stand isolated as an independent element.

In the major work ***The Scream***, powerful expression has been obtained partly by the use of those rhythmical wave-lines contrasted with ribbon-lines typical of Art Nouveau. The road with the wooden fence, which moves diagonally in and up to the left, creates a powerful perspective area which almost breaks the surface of the picture and rushes towards the onlooker, while the soft and curved shapes of the landscape give one a feeling of being sucked into the picture. The strange figure in the foreground makes the angst concrete and personified.

Death in the Sickroom similarly condenses a spiritually-agonising experience: the death of his sister Sophie. Death's ice-cold stillness is effected by the use of simple convincing colour-contrasts: the actors have mask-like faces, and the action is performed on an insistently sloping stage floor. This work shows Munch's first-hand knowledge of the contemporary stylistic tendencies of synthetism and symbolism.

In 1894, for the first time, Munch tried graphic techniques - in the beginning for the sake of variation and to explore in greater depth the subjects he had earlier painted - but soon graphic works became end-products in themselves. He proved to be an innovator in this field, too: thanks to a complete command of the different techniques he quickly reached a unique strength of expression. The copper plate became his first graphic medium and his first portraits quickly attracted general respect. By using all available etching and scratching techniques he attained a richer form of expression. Through a series of experimental and test prints one can follow Munch's procedure in a unique way. In 1895 he extended his graphic productions to the lithographic stone, which was particularly suited to recreating the ***Frieze of Life*** themes in black and white. These themes, with the interaction of wavy lines and flat areas, were, in the lithographic medium, simplified in the Art Nouveau-accentuated way popular at that time.

In Paris in 1896 Munch at long last began to work in wood-cuts,and the simplification process was carried even further, in a quasi-primitive direction. We can clearly see how Munch made the most of the grain of the wood to make a decorative pattern assisted by nature herself. Although Munch's use of wood-cutting was based on Gauguin's wood-cuts, Munch created a modern form of expression which became very important to the further development of the Brücke Group's expressionistic graphics, as it was developed after the turn of the century around the central figure of Ernst

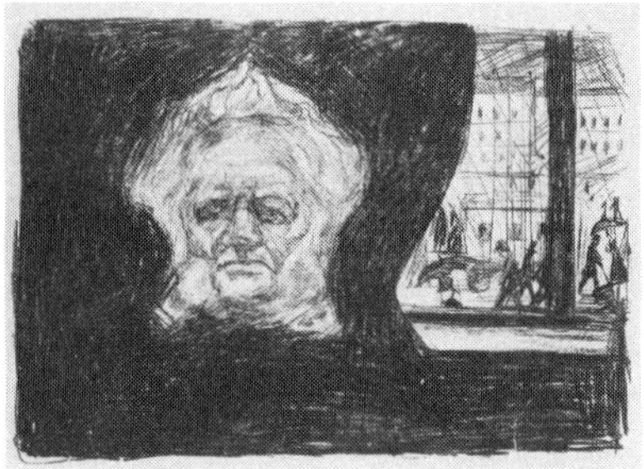

Henrik Ibsen at the Grand Café, 1902 Lithograph

Ludwig Kirchner.

During the years 1896-98 Munch, on the whole, lived in Paris. He was integrated into the artistic and musical milieu in which the one thing the members had in common was admiration for the art of Gauguin and Rodin. Munch was given a commission to illustrate Baudelaire's *Les Fleurs du Mal* - a project which did not come off, however, because the publisher died. He also executed programme posters for Ibsen's *Peer Gynt* and *John Gabriel Borkman* for the Théâtre de l'Oeuvre. He caused a great sensation with several exhibitions of his major works, one of them in the Salon des Indépendants.

In the summer of 1899 Munch went to Northern Italy and Rome where, principally, he studied the major works of Renaissance art. In Paris on his way home, Munch enthusiastically told Julius Meier-Graefe that he had been inspired by Raphael's work and was now going home to create art intended for large wall areas.

Probably the many winter landscapes from the turn of the century were evidence above all of an ambition to create mural compositions. These have a rhythmical and lyrical atmosphere in area, colour and linear movement, and there is hardly any trace of the earlier nervous engagement and restless experimentation. Munch manages to convey an intensely sensitive observation of nature in the classically simplified idiom of synthetist art in the Art Nouveau style. Other paintings in strong colours from this period are ***Metabolism***, ***Melancholy*** (his sister Laura in a room), ***The Dance of Life***, ***Golgotha*** and ***Red Vine*** which signify a temporary end to the ***Frieze of Life*** project.

Much later it was said that the painting ***Metabolism*** was as important to the ***Frieze of Life*** *"as the buckle to a belt"*. He gave an almost mythological-philosophical interpretation of the mystery of life; a naked woman and man stand on either side of the axially-placed tree, its bark cracking, and from the crack a child appears. It depicts the myth of the birth

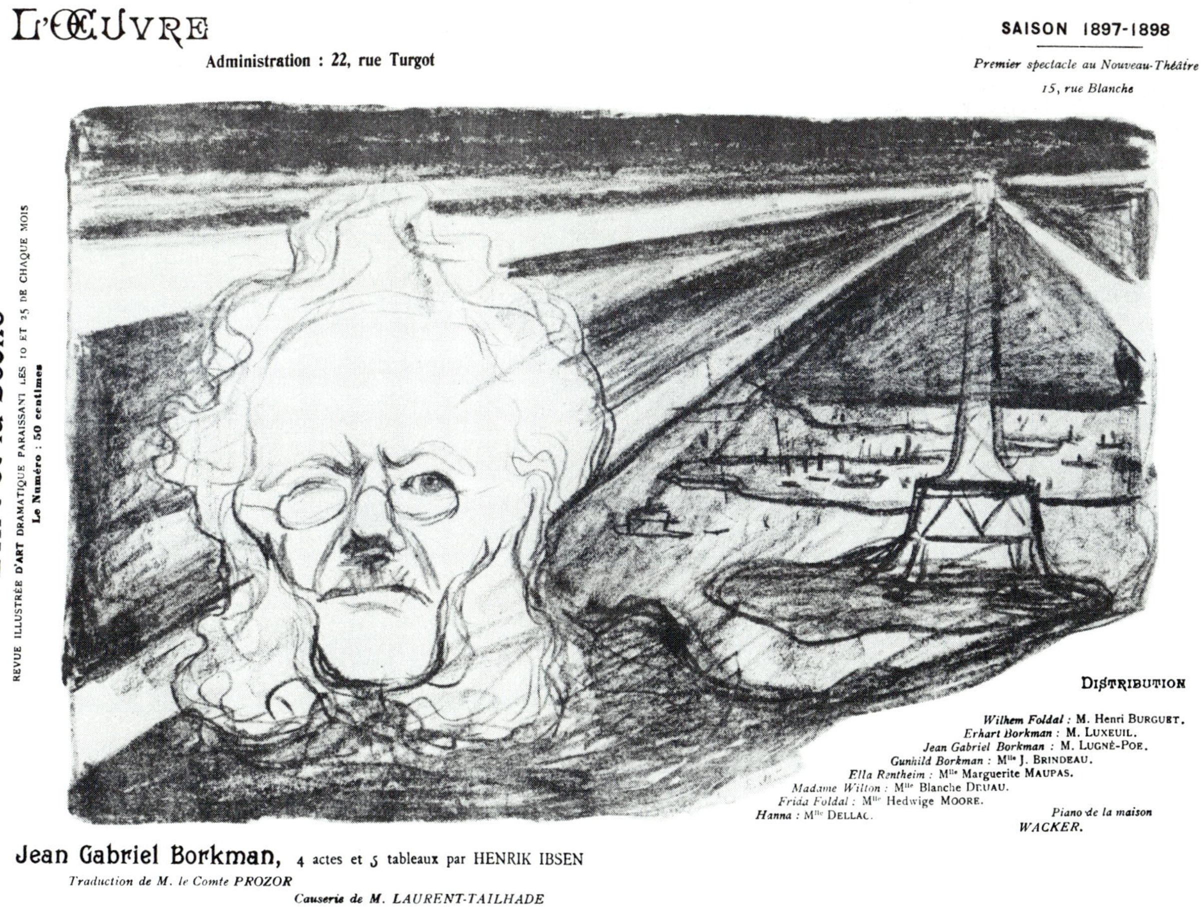

Ibsen with Lighthouse, 1897
Lithograph

of the fertility god Adonis in modern guise.

By pushing the figure of the woman in ***Melancholy*** into a corner of the room, between the landscape outside and the reflection of it on the wall beside her, Munch completely isolates her from the world outside. The bluish landscape is contrasted with the flower on the table in front of her. In Munch's oeuvre, the flower is often repeated as a symbol of art, sucking nourishment from the blood. The melancholy woman, who can also be seen as a symbol of the artist himself, seems to have established a kind of contact with the flower, but not with reality outside.

In 1902 the *Berlin Secession* invited Munch to exhibit, among other works, the ***Frieze of Life***. The collective title of Munch's central theme of love, angst and death is seen historically as a flexible concept, but this exhibition remains the most important basis for understanding what the concept of Munch's project was meant to cover.

The exhibition demonstrated Munch's importance to the young Northern European art movement, and gave him extensive success in Germany. From this time on, and until his breakdown in 1908, Munch lived almost permanently in Germany, where he also took a series of unique photographic self-portraits with a small Kodak camera he had obtained in 1902. These photographic self-portraits were described by Munch himself as "Destiny Photographs"and portray an anguished record of the fundamental loneliness of man.

The paintings he executed in this period were a series of full-length portraits which were well-received. The portraits include Walter Rathenau, Hermann Schlittgen (***The German***) and Marcel Archinard (***The Frenchman***). The models are portrayed with great psychological insight and with concentrated power, without any sign of the nullifying effect of trying to make a hero of the sitter, which traditionally is the tendency for pictures of this type. Munch also painted a series of children's portraits, and he took on some decorative work for, among others, the art patron Max Linde in Lübeck (1902-04): ***Youth on the Beach***, and for Max Reinhardt's new theatre in Berlin (1906-08), and completed a series of landscapes and figure compositions. He often exhibited in the larger German cities, and in Vienna and Paris.

It is difficult to say to what extent Munch influenced subsequent modernism at this period. It is indisputable that the work he produced during the sixteen years between 1892 and 1908 was of vital importance to the development of the expressionist movement in pictorial art, primarily for the Brücke artists in Germany, but also for the Fauves in France.

During these years Munch assumed a more affirmative attitude to life than before, which his major dynamic painting ***Bathing Men*** shows, painted in Warnemünde in the summer of 1907. He also painted a series of genre-influenced themes that summer, where the canvas has been painted partly spontaneously and partly in impasto, as in the earliest paintings by Matisse, where oil paint was pressed onto the canvas in thick layers straight from the tube, as in ***Old Man in Warnemünde*** and ***Children on the Street***. He tried out this technique later in a series of pessimistic themes which were given the collective title of ***The Green Room***. This is evidence of an increasing state of nervousness and deep despair. It is a new and bitter development of the original ***Frieze of Life*** where the elegiac coastline from Åsgårdstrand has been replaced by the interior of a brothel. In five of the pictures in the series, the action is in the same room, a small stage-like room with green wallpaper: ***Zum Süssen Mödel***, ***Desire***, ***Hate***, ***Jealousy*** and ***The Murderess***. The fact that the subject seems so close makes the insistently unpleasant room seem vastly extended, as if it were recorded with a wide-angle lens.

Loneliness is now described in a more desperate and aggressive way than before, and it seems to typify the atmosphere of this whole series. To use a work of art as a means of expressing a feeling of bitterness and loathing, without a moral sideways glance, warns one of something new in pictorial art: a form of *'bad painting'* for which only our generation understands the justification.

Munch also spent that summer of 1908 in Warnemünde, where he took up the *'doppelganger'* theme which is central to German expressionistic art. In the painting ***The Bricklayer and the Mechanic*** a light and a dark male figure walk side by side towards the onlooker. One gets a strong impression that the two figures represent two sides of the same person. In ***The Drowned Child***, the same two figures move into the picture space. Here he also experiments for the first time with the spontaneous introduction of an artistic focal point as we (for instance) find in the transparent horse in the left foreground of the picture, suggested by only a few brush strokes.

After a year of restlessness, nervous problems and alcohol abuse, he had a breakdown in the autumn of 1908. Munch spent the following eight months in Dr Jacobson's mental clinic in Copenhagen.

When he returned to Norway, he settled first in the little coastal town of Kragerø where he began a completely new chapter in his life and he immediately started work on a design for a competition to decorate the Oslo University Hall. In spite of considerable opposition to his suggestions, he won the competition and the murals were ready in 1916. The three central areas in this major work in Norwegian monumental painting, ***History***, ***The Sun***, and ***Alma Mater*** - clearly show new developments in Munch's art, evidence of his renewed encounter with Norwegian Landscape which resulted in a classical simplicity in the composition, and vigorous, spontaneous brush strokes.

While Munch was painting the University decorations, he was also preoccupied with Northern Italian Renaissance art, particularly with Masaccio and Giotto. It is most clearly expressed in ***History*** where the figures are sitting in a space cut out of the cliffs (which was the natural landscape around Kragerø) as if it had been interpreted by one of the earlier Renaissance masters. It has been claimed that Munch partly based this landscape on a drawing Leonardo da Vinci made of the Arno Valley.

The Sun is convincing evidence of the new spontaneity of his brush strokes and becomes a manifestation of Munch's own powerful worship of nature. The new, free and bold strokes can probably be best observed in ***Galloping Horse***. The horse gallops through the snow and sweeps the secondary figures to the side, and runs with terrific power out towards the onlooker. The illusion of movement is obtained by an exaggerated foreshortening, and the impression of dynamism is reinforced by its head, which is tossed to one side. In spite of all the differences, the vitality of movement in Munch's ***Galloping Horse*** can be seen in parallel with the direction of the Italian Futurists. The Futurists, particularly Boccioni, were absorbed by Munch's art, and they shared Munch's enthusiasm for film as a source of inspiration.

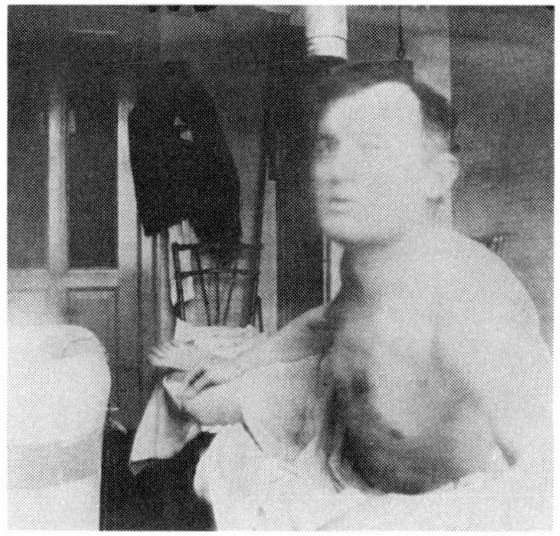

Edvard Munch 'a la Marat', 1908-09 Self portrait

In the painting ***The Yellow Tree Trunk*** a dynamic movement has been added, which faintly reminds one of the medium of film. If one traverses the picture at a certain distance, the perspective seems to change in a peculiar way as if one's glance is continually being attracted along the logs towards the edge of the forest. This foreshortening technique refers directly back to Munch's photographic self-portrait taken in the bathroom at Dr Jacobson's clinic, where his naked body, strongly foreshortened, seems to shoot out towards the onlooker.

At the famous Sonderbund Exhibition in Cologne in 1912 (the intention of which was to give a complete survey of the most important movements in modern art) Munch was given his own large room, and was thus presented as the contemporary artist who had had the greatest significance in its development.

The year after, at the Autumn Exhibition in Berlin, he and Picasso, the only foreign artists invited, were given a room each. The aim was to distinguish them as being of paramount importance to young German art. But while the continuing development of modern painting is characterized by free construction of fragments of reality - as we see in Cubism and Futurism - or, as in Kandinsky, by forms without direct reference to the outer world - to Munch the outer reality became the fulcrum of his art. He now created a whole series of pictures on the theme of the working man's life, including for example ***Workmen in the Snow*** (1902), ***Man in a Cabbage Field*** 1916, ***Workmen on their way Home*** 1914, which can be looked upon as a symbol of the advance of a new era, not in a political sense, but of new powers forcing their way ahead. The angle of incidence of the subject and the out-of-proportion central figure also provide an association with the movement and distortion of the medium of film.

In the 1920's and 30's Munch retired to his property at Ekely outside Oslo, where he avoided all social contact apart from a few close friends. He was completely absorbed in his work and was enormously prolific. In 1922 he completed the murals for the Freia Chocolate Factory in Oslo, a series of paintings which were part of the new, positive version of the ***Frieze of Life***, and are evidence of a happy and life-affirming attitude.

Most of his output from this period comprises landscapes, portraits and compositions which give evidence of an intense response to the surrounding world, and at the same time show a continuing development of style. Munch painted a series of landscapes including a group of bluish pictures of winter nights viewed from Ekely. Most of these pictures are characterised by harmony and stability. The foregrounds are occupied by long human shadows which give the scenes an irrational and dreamlike atmosphere. In ***Starlit Night*** the picture space is built up with the help of a set of '*sphere segments*' into a firm and logical construction. A powerful light falls over the snow in the middle-distance, and over the town in the background lies a yellow sea of light which meets the blue of the sky in a violet stripe.

Munch's drawings, gouaches and watercolours, as well as the abundant sketchbooks, represent an enormous variation on all those themes he took up in his paintings and graphic works. But surprisingly, he rarely develops them to what we would call exhibitable work. This is remarkable as his many and varied drawings have a feeling of immediacy and freshness about them, and his watercolours have a glow of colour which takes one by surprise. We can almost feel how his thoughts and ideas glow from behind the fine recordings of visual impressions. The following story shows how unorthodoxly he often used his drawings as studies to investigate new visual experiences.

In May 1930 a bloodvessel burst in Munch's right eye, and caused almost total blindness as his left eye was already weak. The cause was high blood pressure and overwork; to put it bluntly: old age. When the illness retreated in the month of August, and there was a relative improvement, Munch again used his illness as material for his art. In study after study one can follow how Munch, with the persistence and will of a scientist, experiments and observes the disturbances of his sight which the illness had caused. Carefully he wrote down his observations, giving dates and times, distance from the sheet of paper and from the window, the type of spectacles etc. The result was a series of drawings built up with the help of spectral colours grouped together in concentric circles. He portrayed the projection in the interior of his damaged eye on a sheet of paper. In the centre he drew the damaged part, often in the form of a bird. Some of the drawings were given an almost abstract character, and glowed in shining colours which until then had been unknown in Munch's art.

During 1932-35 Munch again took up the themes of his earlier ***Frieze of Life***, executed in brilliant colours, as one can see in ***Two Women on the Beach***. He himself called these repetitions *"radical copies"*. Munch was probably influenced by the large official review of young German art in Oslo in January 1932. The Brucke artists were amongst those represented, and particularly in Karl Schmidt-Rottluff's works, colour was treated brutally.

Self-Portrait Between Clock and Bed, 1940-42 Oil on canvas

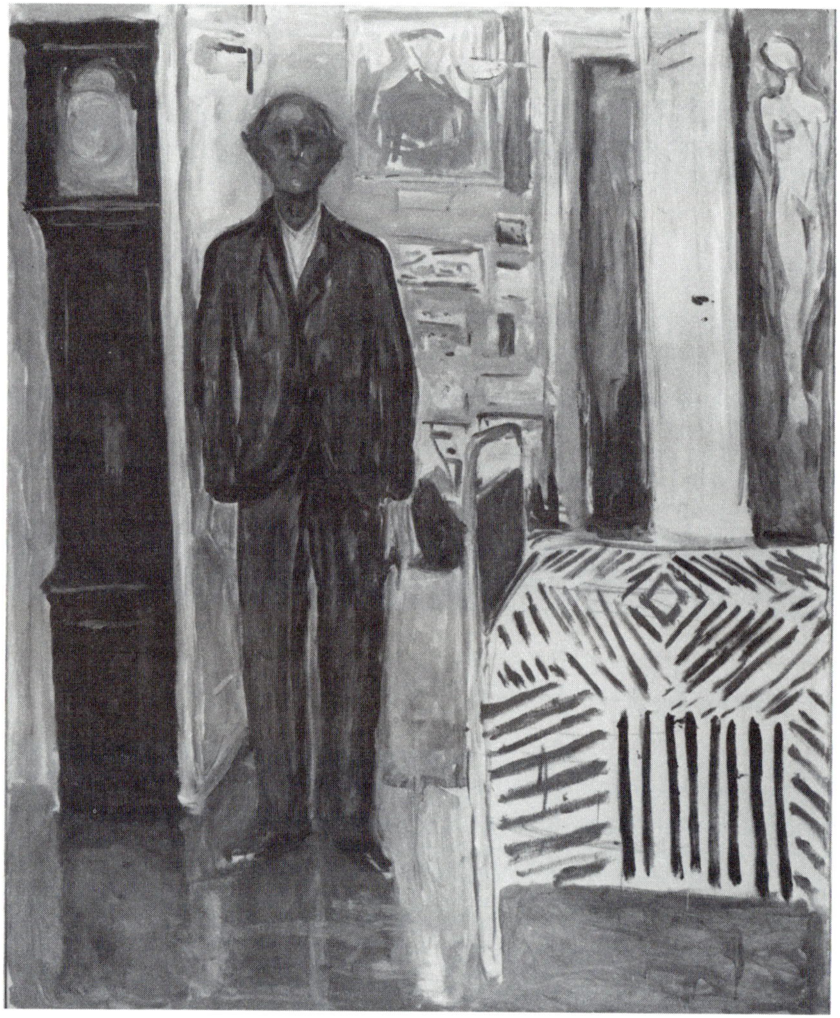

All through his life Munch revealed himself in his art, and the recurrent series of self-portraits are examples of his search for self-knowledge. In ***Self-Portrait*** 1886, he looks self-importantly at us out of the corner of his eye; it is the young man who is aware of his talent, the painter of ***The Sick Child*** who in this portrait uses the same technique as in his major works. In ***Self-Portrait in Hell*** the yellow body is strongly lit from below, while a threatening shadow expresses an unmistakeable angst. The mask-like features of the face, and the background filled with contrasts, provide the raison d'être for the title. A comparison with a series of before and after studies for the painting makes even the naturalistic starting- point clear: Munch's face was sunburned, but his body was pale.

Self-Portrait with Wine can similarly be explained by a series of photographic self-portraits, which he himself calls *"destiny photographs"*, 1902-1908. In a desperate period of his life, both personally and artistically, he studies himself in his loneliness in small hotel rooms - in the mirror as well as through the eye of the camera. It is, incidentally, important to note that at the same time as referring to his greyish-coloured photographs, he makes the colours in his paintings speak: ie. clear, spectral colours as we see them on the brushes he holds in his hand in ***Self-Portrait with Brushes***.

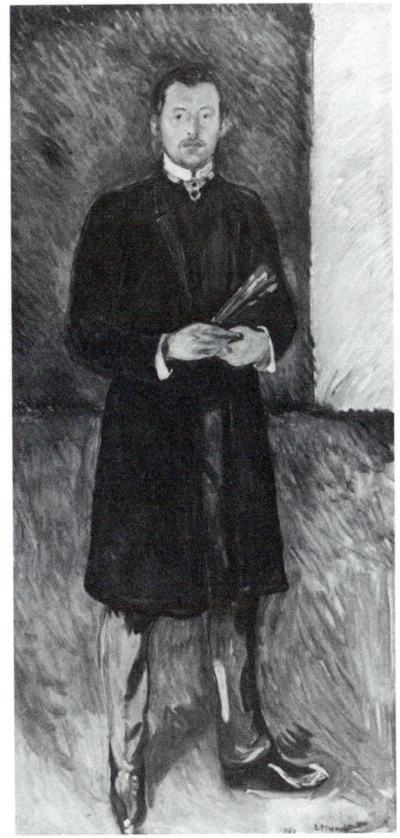

Self-Portrait With Brushes, 1904
Oil on canvas

Finally, one should mention the large group of self-portraits from the last two decades of his life, where year by year he was monitoring his own mental and physical decline towards death. Ruthlessly, almost contemptuously, he exposes the old man's condition in paintings and watercolours. In some of these his fear of death is quite tangible.

In ***Self-Portrait Between Clock and Bed*** he poses between two symbols of death: the clock and the bed. He stands, very lonely, in the foreground of a strongly-lit room filled with the works of art which were his life. Munch is merciless in his studies of himself in ***Self-Portrait at 2.15 in the Morning*** where he is staring ahead, half-raising himself from a chair. Behind the chair we can perceive death as a dark shadow which has

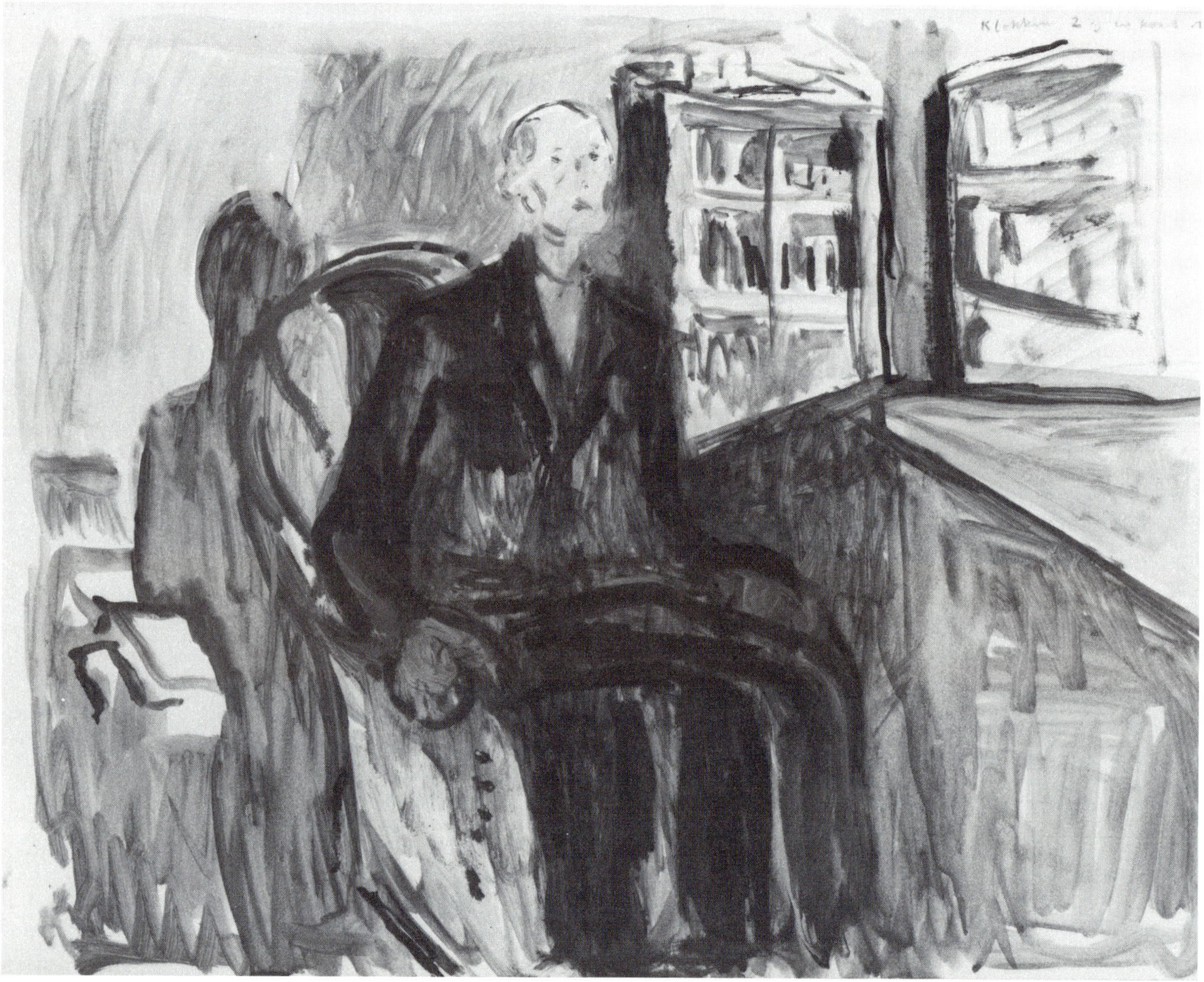

Self-portrait at 2.15 am, 1940-44
Gouache

followed him all through his life. With a weakened body and a skull which was already marked by death, Munch is staring up towards the light. With the utmost consistency he has created a life's work which not only lets the serious problems of the turn of the century live further into our time, but also tells us of aspects of human existence which can hardly be conveyed in words.

Arne Eggum

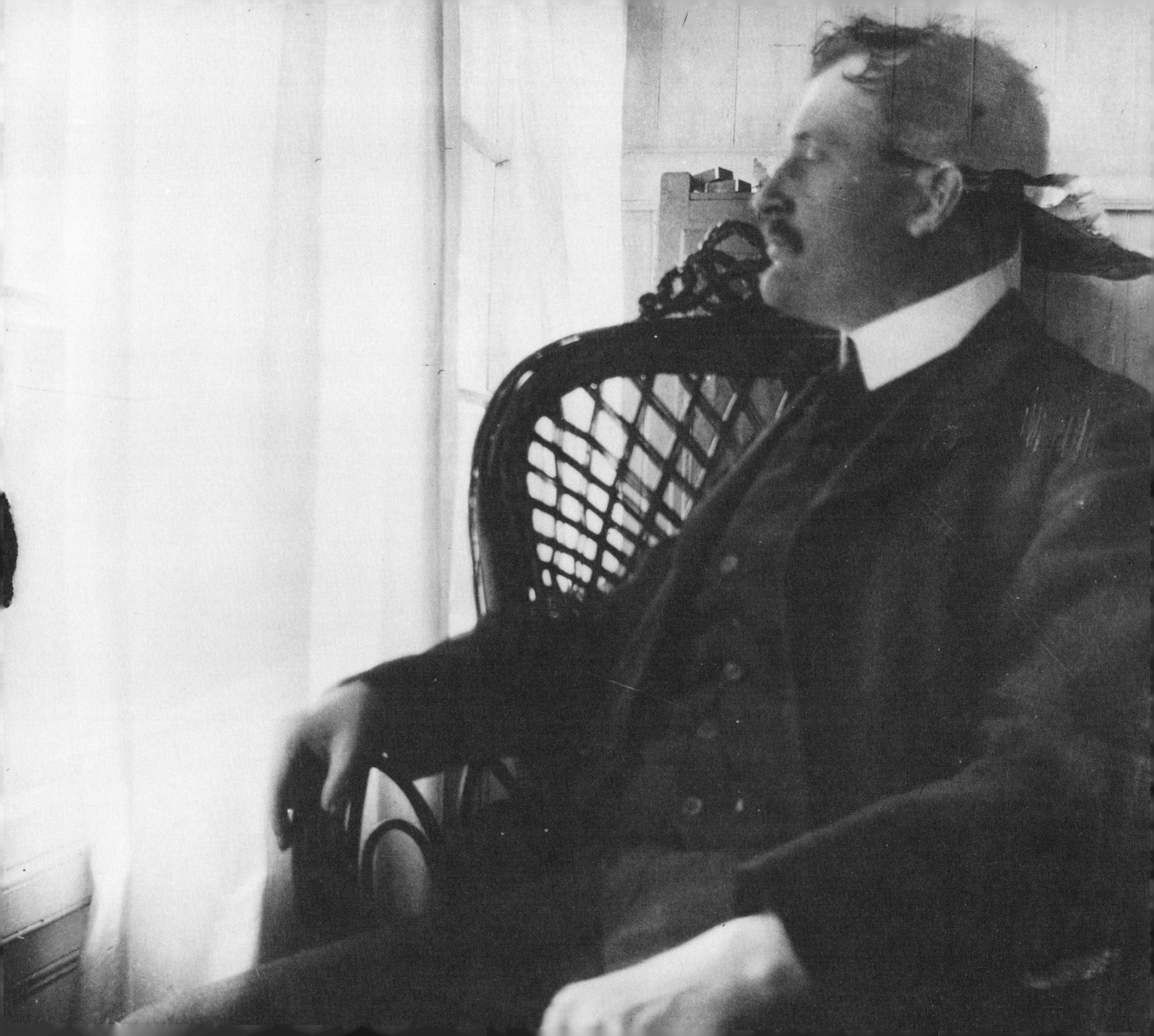

Edvard Munch and photography

One of the most surprising aspects of the exhibition '*Paintings from Photographs*' in Munich in 1970 was Edvard Munch's use of photography as an aid to and source for some of his pictures. In this respect Munch's own work as an amateur photographer was of peripheral interest, although Professor J A Schmidt, referring to Eisenwerth, remarked in the introduction to the exhibition catalogue: "*Munch is technically so imperfect, but also so marvellously unconventional in his production of life studies and portraits as to show a psychological insight which cannot otherwise be found in photographs from that period.*"

In the article '*Munch's Photographic Studies*' the same author expands on the topic some years later, but concludes with his original point that Munch's own photographs were amateur pictures whose obvious aesthetic qualities were accidental and not due to conscious effort.

Eisenwerth also took it for granted that Munch's repeated use of double exposures was purely due to lapse of memory on the artist's part, that is, that he had forgotten to wind on the film between exposures. If on the other hand one analyses Munch's photographs primarily as expressions of experimental intent, the material can be understood on its own merits and in its historical context.

In Kristiania in the 19th century, when Munch was training to be an artist, photography was accepted as an aid for artists when it was a matter of objective reproduction of reality. Christian Krohg, for example, Munch's teacher, painted over photographs in preparation for his major work '*Albertine at the Police Doctor's*'.

While some young artists cultivated photographically-inspired realistic painting, the photograph inspired others to the contrary: a concentration on what was unique to painting: colour and the various painterly disciplines. Among the latter, Munch went furthest in emphasising a subjective response to reality.

A visit to Copenhagen in 1888, and the influences which could be

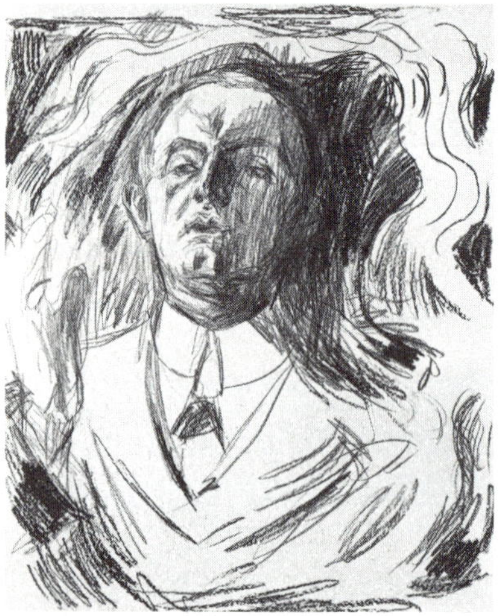

Self-Portrait with Cigarette, 1908-09 Lithograph

absorbed there, undoubtedly contributed to his attitude to his rôle as an artist. Apart from Scandinavian painting (and photography) at the Nordic Exhibition he could familiarise himself with French art at the large contemporary French exhibition, where amongst others, the Impressionists were copiously represented. It was then that Munch's characterisation of his art as a diametric contrast to photographic realism was formulated: *"We want something different from the purely photographic representation of nature. Nor is it to paint pretty pictures to be put on parlour walls. We wish to try, if we can, to build a foundation of art to give to people. An art that reaches and grips. Art created from one's heart's blood."*

With a collection of paintings created from such an aesthetic, Munch arrived in Berlin in 1892, and his subsequent exhibition there gave him European fame from then on. Among other things, it brought about his friendship with August Strindberg who was also staying in Berlin. During this period (1892 -1894) and later in Paris (1896 - 1898) Strindberg was more preoccupied with his photographic experiments than with his own activity as a writer. At the same time, he painted with intense spontaneity, naturalistic paintings which he himself thought were equal to Munch's. Munch, meanwhile, expressed his own literary ambitions at this period. The belief that nature itself can disclose its fundamental laws with the artist as a medium, as Strindberg expressed it in his essay '*Concerning Chance in Artistic Creation*' (1894), also throws light on the spontaneously experimental character of Munch's mature art.

Munch's famous painting ***Self-Portrait with Cigarette*** from 1895, with its strangely loaded atmosphere and distinctive illumination from below, bears a striking resemblance to a couple of Strindberg's photographic self-portraits from Gersau (1886). In Berlin, Strindberg had a visiting card made with precisely this motif - which Munch must have known particularly well.

Strindberg is standing in the same pose, holding the cigarette in the same manner as Munch, and here too the illumination is clearly from below.

The light distorts the features of both men so that the beard, the mouth and the eyes appear surprisingly equal in value. There is something diffuse and ghostlike in both the photograph and the painting.

It is also quite fascinating to discover the similarity between Strindberg's strange celestography (a kind of direct photography of the star-studded firmament, taken without the use of a lens) and the glittering firmament in Munch's art from the 1890's, particularly in the etched variations on the theme ***Attraction*** (1895). In some of his work of this time, Munch created graphic portraits based on photography, including, for example, those of Stéphane Mallarmé, Knut Hamsun and Henrik Ibsen. But it was not until he obtained a small Kodak camera in Berlin in 1902, that Munch's own photographs became an essential aid to his art.

In a letter from Berlin dated 14.02.1902 to his aunt, Karen Bjølstad, Munch refers to his first amateur photographs of January/February 1902: *"Herewith two photographs taken with a small camera I have obtained for myself. You can see that I have almost got rid of my moustache."*

One of these photographs is most likely the one in which he is shown sitting on a big suitcase in his studio in Lützowstrasse 82 in Berlin. He is surrounded by the paintings which resulted in his decisive breakthrough in the Prussian capital. Two almost identical versions of the subject still exist. One of the photographs was framed by his aunt and hung above the settee in the family's flat. In it Munch can clearly be seen holding a broad-brimmed dark hat in his right hand. The dim outline of the hat suggests that Munch has been moving it. In the other photograph, he appears more in profile and the hat can scarcely be seen. Such a photograph must have needed an exposure of about half a minute, and Munch must have used the hat to cover the lens for the time he took to sit down on the case, and later to have covered it again as soon as he thought the film was sufficiently exposed. The fact that the hat was dark and matt made it particularly suited to the purpose.

Presumably one of the reasons why Munch took two photographs of

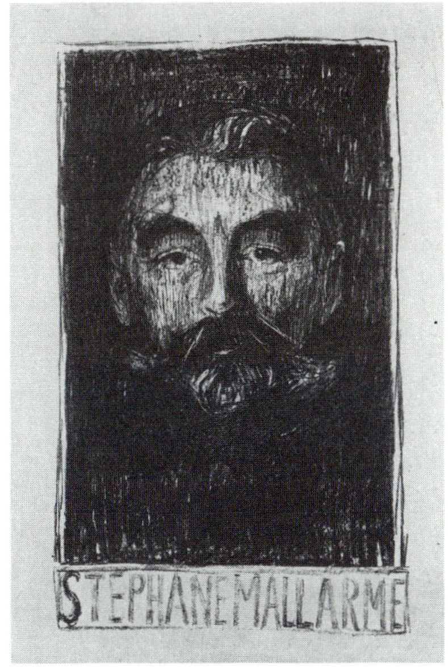

Stéphane Mallarmé, 1896
Lithograph

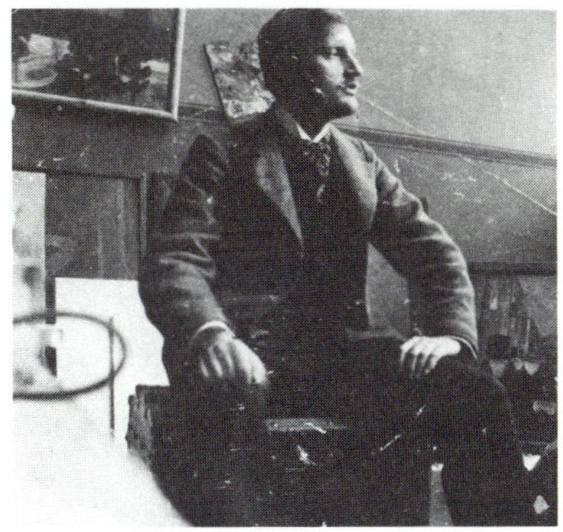

Munch in his studio,
Lutzowstrasse 82, Berlin, 1902

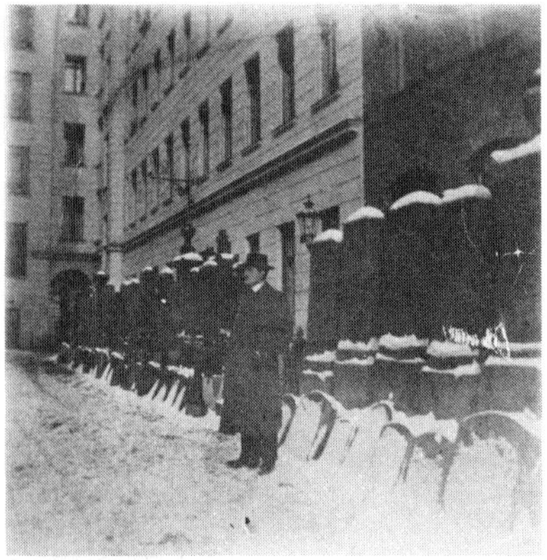

Munch, Berlin, 1902, taken by Albert Kollman

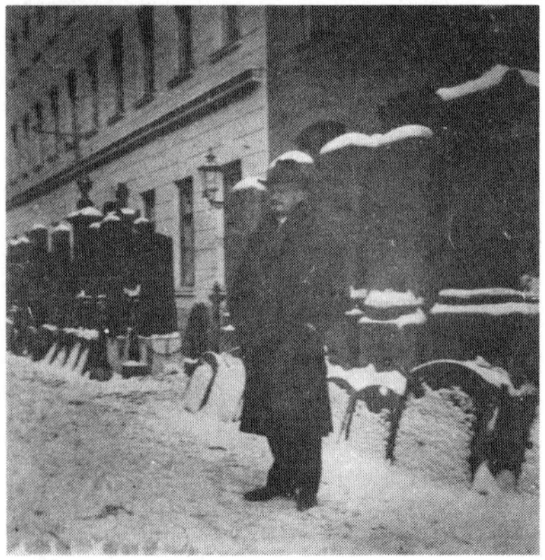

Kollman, Berlin, 1902, taken by Munch

the same subject was that he was experimenting with various exposure times. The full-face portrait is slightly over-exposed in comparison with the profile picture.

An existing series of these studio photographs, all taken about the same time, show that Munch systematically photographed his new surroundings.

In one photograph a life model, with long hair and black stockings, stands behind a table in front of the painting ***Woman in Three Phases*** (1894). This model was the basis for at least two subjects: the painting ***Standing Model*** and the lithograph ***Sin***. These both therefore should be dated back to 1902. In all the photographs the walls, the floor and the table are strewn with oils and graphic works, both old and new.

Although most of the photographs can be dated with reasonable certainty or placed in roughly chronological order, a few must be given tentative dates. There are, for example, two photographs respectively of Munch and the occultist Albert Kollmann against a background of snow-covered gravestones in a back yard, probably in Berlin.

Kollman's photograph of Munch is the more conventional one, from a compositional point of view, whilst Munch has symbolically placed Kollman at the intersection of a dark and a light building. It is tempting to believe that these photographs are among the very first taken with Munch's new camera in January/February 1902, the moment when they came together in what they felt to be a predestined friendship.

Shortly afterwards, in September 1902, Munch had one of the fingers of his left hand shot off and another damaged, during the definitive ending of his love affair with Tulla Larsen. An X-ray taken at the Christiania Rontgen Institute shows the bullet in his finger. In his notes from that date one can read with what desperation he viewed what he later called his '*hand of destiny*' after the operation:

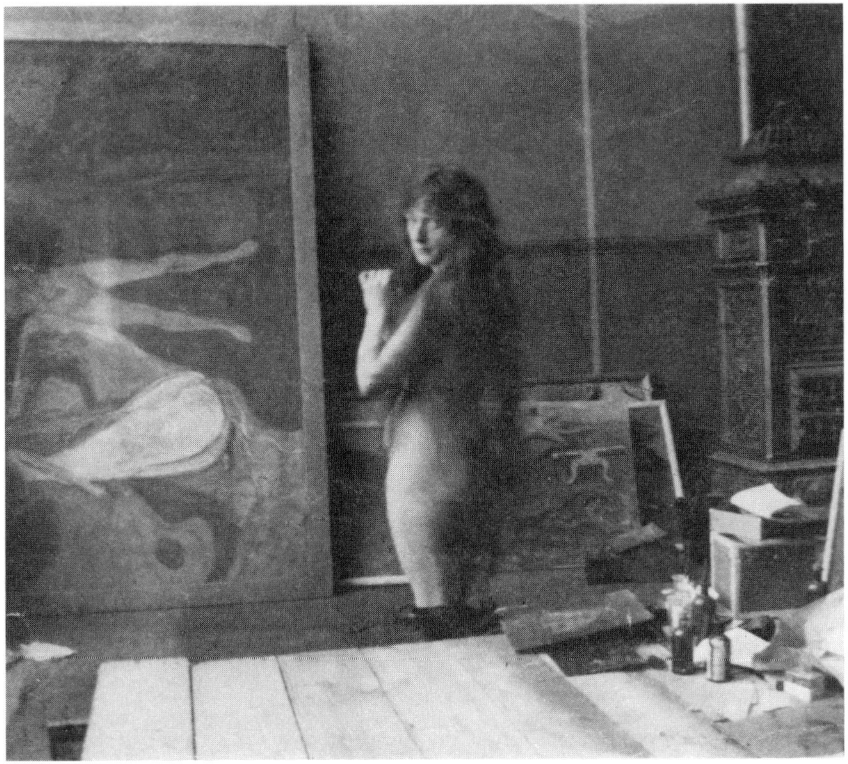

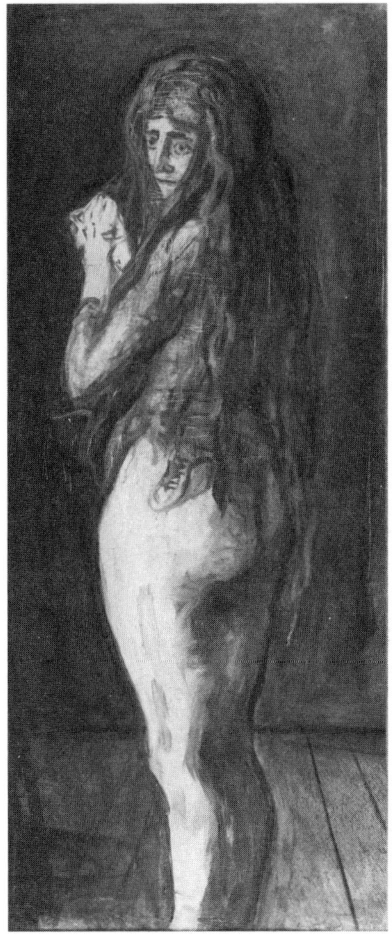

Standing Nude, 1902 Oil on canvas

Left: Model posing in studio, Berlin, 1902

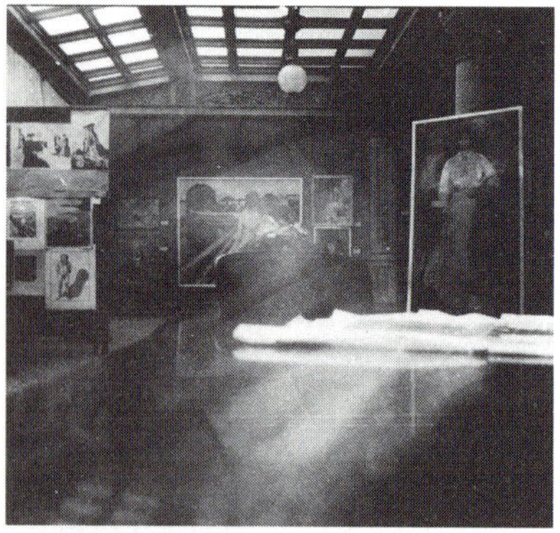

Munch's exhibition at Blomqvist, Kristiania, 1902

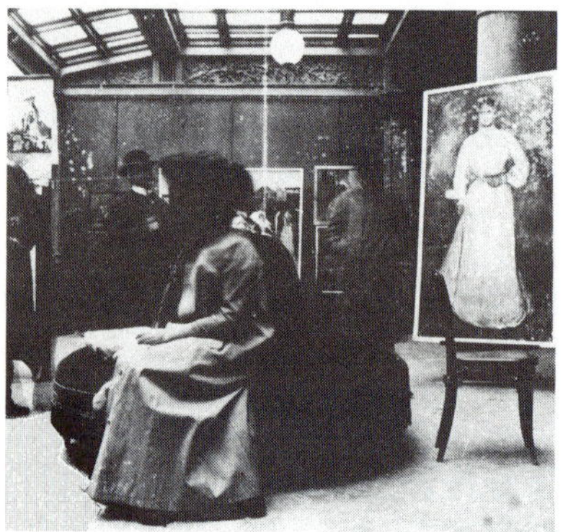

"- *the bandage on the hand was taken off*

- *a shudder went through him*

- *a monstrosity*

- *a terrible stunted limb*

- *was his previously well-formed hand*

- *his previous helper in his work*

- *stunted, hideous and useless*"

The event became a traumatic obsession for Munch and serves as an explanation of the difficulties leading to his breakdown in 1908. In his literary notes, plays, lithographic series and - as we shall also see - in photography, he dwells on the humiliation , which also became the raw material for the bitter subjects in his paintings of this period, which is otherwise marked by a symbolic affirmation of life, and strong, pure colours.

The comprehensive exhibition of his recent works at Blomqvist's gallery in Kristiania (which opened on 24th September 1902, immediately after he was discharged from hospital) became for Munch an anticlimax to the international recognition he received in Berlin the same Spring and Summer. The exhibition was at first very badly attended. After an anonymous insertion in the paper '*Aftenposten*' - "*We will go on strike*"(17. 10. 1902) with a public appeal to boycott the exhibition of "*trash*"and "*daubings*", the public crowded in. In the satirical magazine '*Tyrihans*' (17.10. 1902) the artist Ragnvald Blix commented on the two events in two joint caricatures, one showing part of the exhibition room before the *'advertisement insertion'*, with only the artist's shadow as spectator. The other drawing showed the anonymous crowd moving through the exhibition room with downcast eyes. In two complementary photographs of the same part of the exhibition room Munch seems to have commented on Blix's caricature. One photograph shows the room empty, without anybody there except possibly the artist's own shadow. A long exposure time explains this effect. Probably by placing the camera on a highly-polished table, the works of art and the ceiling were mirrored in the photograph. The interesting lighting effect, which seems to shine in two directions, suggests that during the exposure Munch fanned an object in front of the lens, or he himself may have moved in front of the camera. The shadow, which was thrown onto the portrait of a woman, must have been Munch's. In the other photograph we can see the public moving past the pictures like hazy ghosts. These two photographs were placed one above the other in an album, further underlying the analogy with Blix's caricatures.

One of the photographs shows his aunt, Karen Bjølstad, sitting, and his sister Inger, standing, in front of a row of houses opposite a park in Kristiania. The two figures have merged into one strange combined shape cut by a landing. The same two models had earlier been depicted in a similar position in the painting ***Mother and Daughter*** (1897) and in the woodcut ***Two Women on the Beach*** (1898). Munch demonstrates that this silhouette-like form, which he had already taken the opportunity to use in ***Death in the Sick Room*** could also be repeated in a photograph. Incidentally, it is worth noting that the inspiration for ***Death in the Sick Room*** probably came from the Belgian painter Fernand Knopff, in particular from his painting ***Memoires*** which is based on the frozen effect of photography.

In the first half of November 1902 Munch went to Lübeck, among other places, to produce a folio of prints for his first big patron, the eye-specialist Dr Max Linde, with his house and family as subjects.

It is evident from a letter from Dr Linde to Munch at the beginning of 1903, that Munch took a number of photographs during his stay there that winter: *"Your amateur photographs are splendid. Pity that you forgot to change, so that Danaide and Burghthor are on the same plate."*

The photographs to which Dr Linde was referring have been lost, but a photograph from Dr Linde's home has been preserved. It shows Munch's painting ***The Operation*** (1902-03), wherein the artist is depicted lying

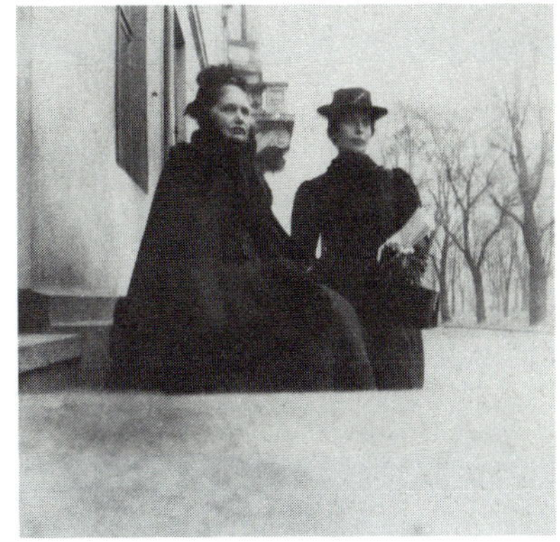

Munch's Aunt Karen and sister Inger, 1902

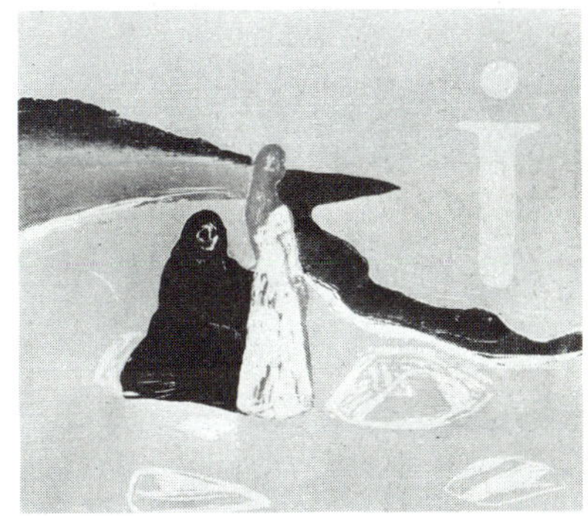

Two Women on the Beach, 1898 Colour Woodcut

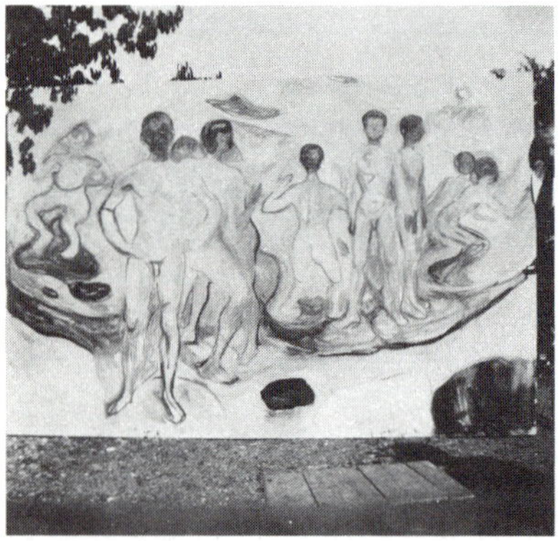

'Bathing Boys' in the garden Åsgårdstrand, 1904

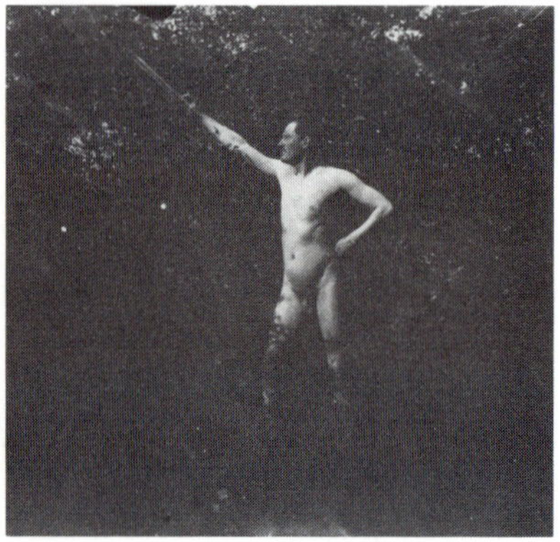

Munch posing, Åsgårdstrand, 1903

stretched-out naked while the revolver bullet which damaged his hand in September 1902 is being removed.

After the big break-through in Berlin with, among others, the exhibition of the ***Frieze of Life*** in a prominent place at the Sculpture Hall at the Berlin-Secession in 1902, Munch altered the course of his art and cultivated a brilliantly-coloured, life-affirming style of painting.

During the summer of 1904, which Munch again spent at Åsgårdstrand, his camera was constantly used; this included taking photographic self-portraits in the nude. Munch was now working on a painting of monumental dimensions of bathing men (which strangely enough was given the title of ***Bathing Boys***).

There are a couple of photographs of himself in the nude, clearly a study for the figure in the foreground.

One of Munch's friends, Christian Gierløff, writes about this summer in his biography of Munch: *"The sun had been hot all day, and we enjoyed it being hot. Munch had painted a little on his bathing picture, but most of the day we had been lying wearied by the sun, in deep hollows in the sand, between big boulders, down by the edge of the fiord, and we let our bodies absorb all the sun we could get. Nobody asked for bathing costumes......"*

In one of the photographs Munch's pose is almost identical to that of his self-portrait, which was only given the additional title *'In Hell'* much later. It was probably painted the year before, in 1903, when it was first exhibited. In both the painting and the photograph it can clearly be seen that Munch's face was sunburnt. The powerful illumination from below is equal to that of the photograph. The concentrated atmosphere of angst, however, is apparent only in the painting.

Another two photographs from the garden at Åsgårdstrand were probably taken in the autumn of 1904, just before the exhibition at Blomqvist's opened on the 16th of October. To judge from the titles in the catalogue, all the paintings seen on the photograph were exhibited. In one of

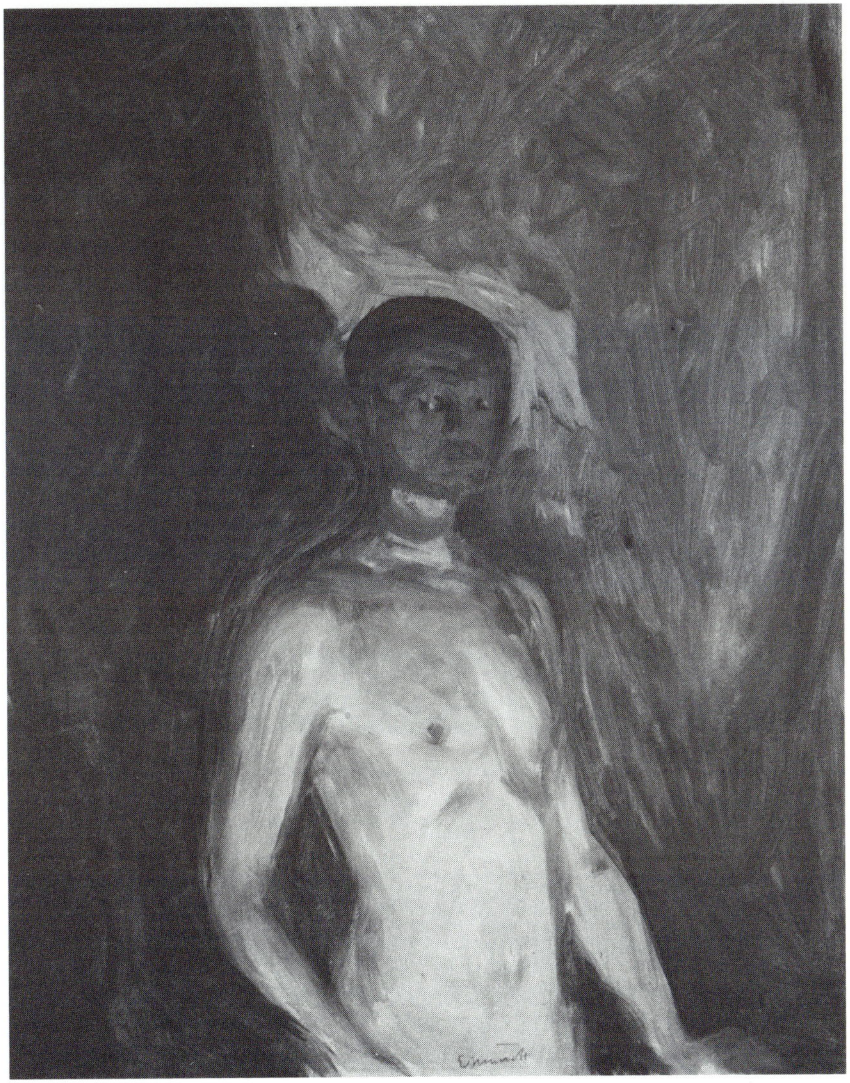

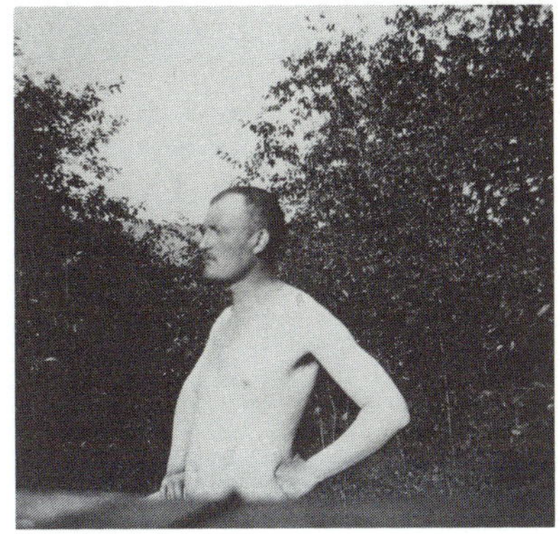

Munch posing, Åsgårdstrand, 1904

Self-Portrait in Hell, 1903 Oil on canvas

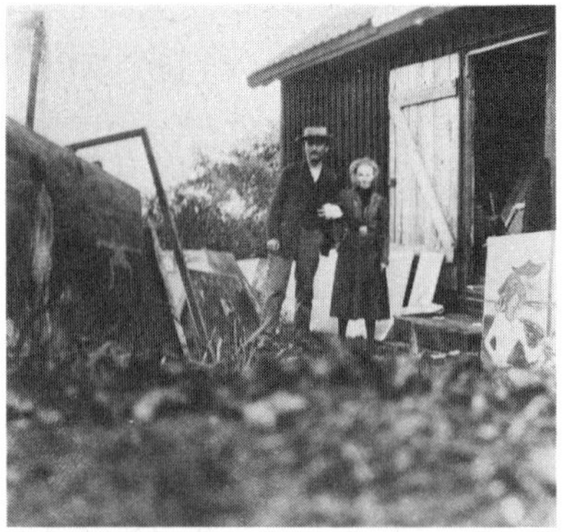

Munch with unidentified girl, Åsgårdstrand, 1904

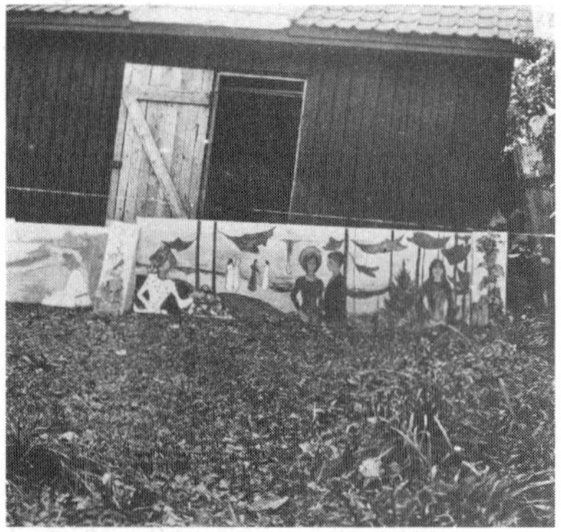

Paintings from the Linde Frieze, Åsgårdstrand, 1904

the photographs Munch can be seen with his hand bandaged, holding the arm of a young model. In August 1904 he had been involved in a fight in Copenhagen with the writer Haukland. The bandaged hand was probably a result of that fight.

The other photograph shows three paintings from the frieze which he painted at the request of Dr Linde in Lübeck. It was placed against an outside wall of the studio. The low perspective and the indistinct foreground suggest that it was taken with the camera standing on a low object.

In a letter from Ludvig Ravensberg, dated Åsgårdstrand 20th November, 1904, we read that Munch brought his camera to Kristiania that autumn. He asked his friend to help him find the camera as he must have left it behind in a cafe.

In a fascinating photographic self-portrait taken in his little house at Åsgårdstrand we can observe that Munch had the same short haircut that he had in the summer of 1904. This makes it likely that it originates from that period. It had been taken from such a short distance that the features are unclear.

A lithographic caricature (1903) can be seen on the wall depicting how Munch was attacked by the '*poodle*', Sigurd Bødtker, while the '*enemy*' were sitting applauding in the background, among them Tulla Larsen and Gunnar Heiberg. The light from behind is cut by a curtain, which has been moved slightly during exposure but the light from the side seems to have been carefully considered.

In another photograph, probably taken about 1906, Munch is sitting in an unidentified, sparsely-furnished room with an unmade bed in the background. The chair which appears to come through the artist as well as the diffuse atmospheric effect, shows that Munch had moved during exposure; it is not a question of double exposure in the ordinary sense.

The artist's despair and the reason for it is symbolically expressed both in the close-up self-portrait from the house at Åsgårdstrand, with the

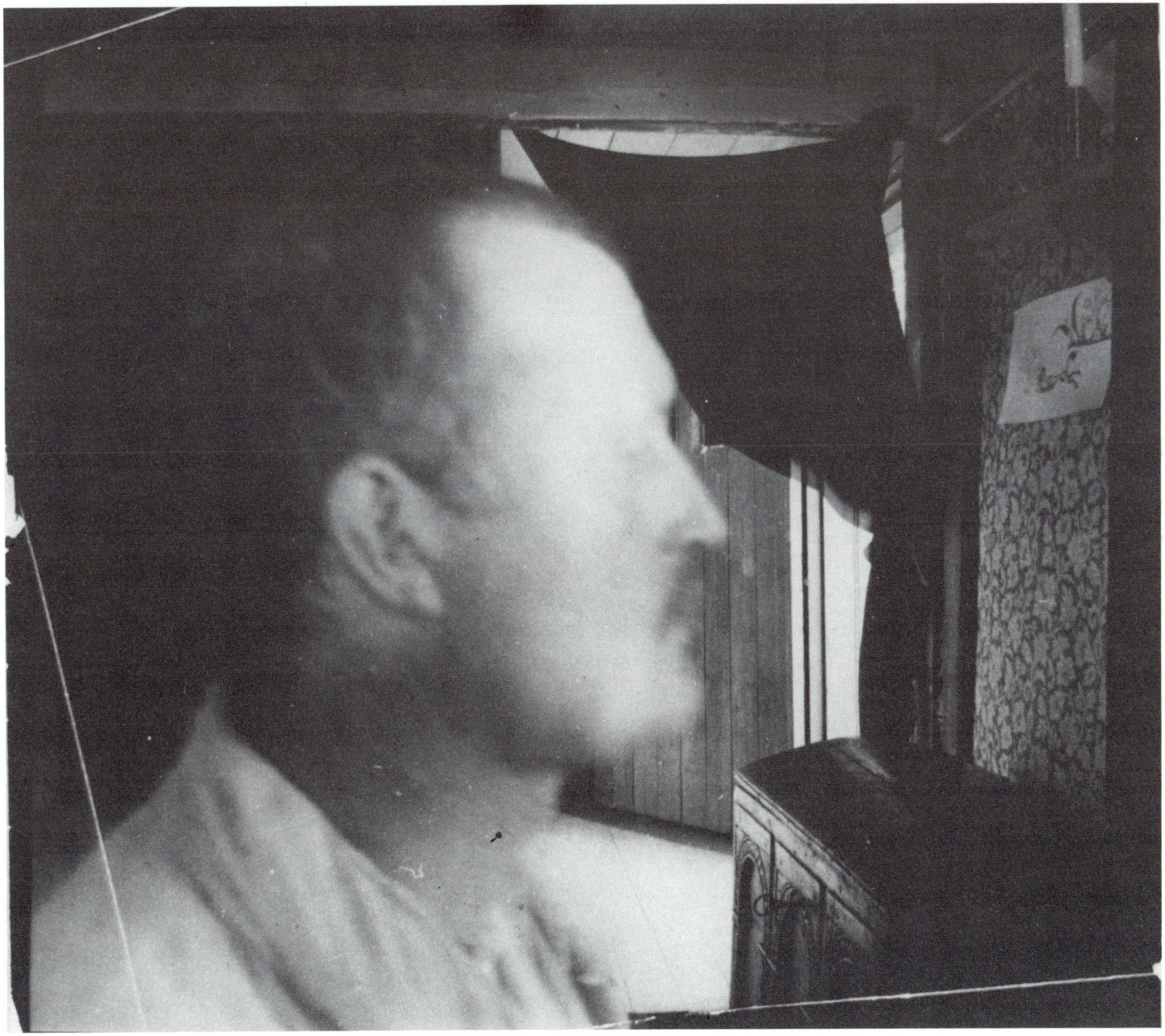

Munch in his house at Åsgårdstrand, 1904

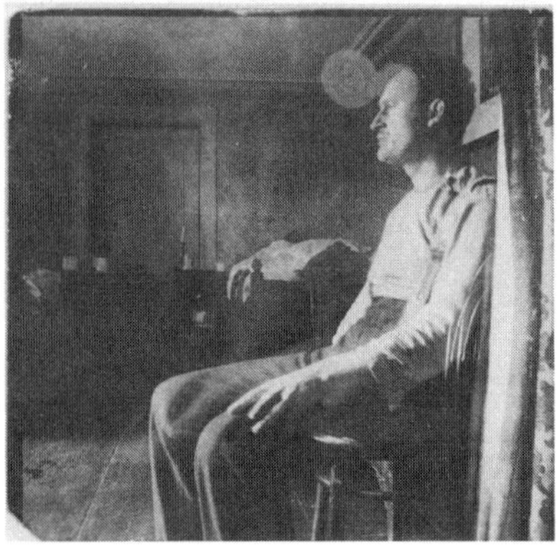

Munch in an unidentififed room on the Continent, probably 1906

lithograph of the '*enemy*' on the wall, and the exposed finger in the photograph. The photographs derive an existential character in a literal way, when Munch comments on his own situation through his photographic documentation of significant events.

A note in a diary from 1943 makes it clear that Munch, at the age of 80, was quite conscious of the meaning of these photographs: *"Folders and clips containing the 'Destiny Photographs' from 1902/08 have been placed in a suitcase. A photograph of me from 1943- with the hand uncovered - will be added."*

A later repetition from 1943 of the typical interior pictures from 1902 to 1908 has been preserved, and it shows Munch sitting with the *hand of destiny* clearly seen; this must have been the photograph mentioned which was "*to be added*". However, this photograph was taken by a professional photographer.

It is reasonable to assume that the photographs Munch named *Destiny Photographs* include a relatively continuous series of pessimistic photographic self-portraits of pronounced symbolic character and an experimental stamp. They all show Munch sitting in a room, and are characterised by a translucent effect: the space behind the artist shines more or less clearly through him. The diffuse atmosphere in the photographs can be said to be analogous with the way he simultaneously formed the atmosphere in his paintings. Munch himself attributed a similar effect in his paintings to a play of luminous colours.

According to Ludvig Ravensberg's diary, December 1909, he said: *"There is something in my pictures I cannot get over - something almost luminous, ghostlike."*

As we have seen, Munch experimented with his first photographic self-portraits by opening and closing the lens with the help of his own dark hat.

For generations professional photographers have opened and closed the lenses of their heavy cameras in the same way. Munch must have found the haziness, which inevitably arose when he moved, exciting from an artistic point of view. At any rate we discover the same effect in a series of photographs taken in various connections over a period of more than seven years.

It therefore seems obvious that Munch tried to get this effect by consciously moving in front of the lens, relating his photography to his other artistic activities.

If we study the interior photographs with *the hand of destiny* from about 1906, more closely, we can plainly see the translucent effect. The two circles in front of the head in one copy, which are perhaps due to some development fluid being spilt on it, seem to have been *repeated* in the form of strong colour marks in ***Self-Portrait with Bottle of Wine*** from 1906, a painting which probably was inspired by this photograph.

The same subject, a self-portrait sitting alone in a room, is repeated in a photograph, perhaps as a supplementary study for the ***Self-Portrait with Bottle of Wine***.. Munch is sitting, apparently depressed, in a rather dark room, looking towards the light. The hands, which are clearly in focus, are clasped. In another photograph some circles of light have formed on the wall near the window. The effect of the illumination gives Munch a ghost-like appearance. In a unique print of 1907 a photograph of Munch sitting in a wicker chair in the conservatory in Am Strom in Warnemünde has a strange, unreal lighting-effect which produces a charged atmosphere. The wooden wall shines through the artist as if he were having an X-ray taken, and *the hand of destiny* is lying clearly exposed on his left thigh. Although the subject may appear relaxed and free from the depressive atmosphere which was seen earlier, the illumination contributes to a disquieting mood.

A photographic life-study, in front of a bed, covers a series of painted and graphic versions of the subject executed up to and including 1906, with the title ***Weeping Girl***. In the photographs there is also a fascinating effect: a woman standing in profile in front of a bed, nude, with her head bowed.

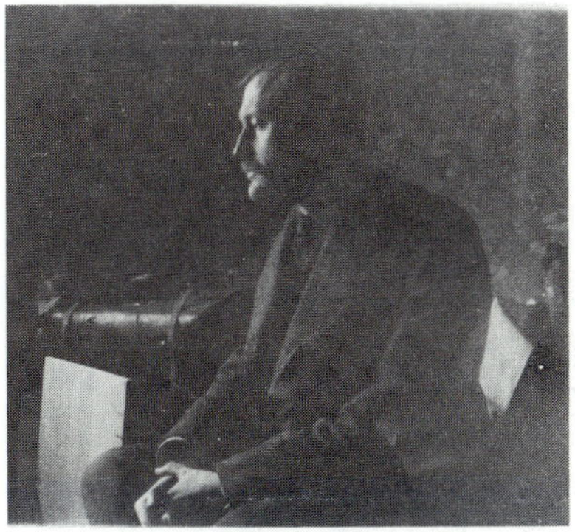

Munch in an unidentified room, probably 1906

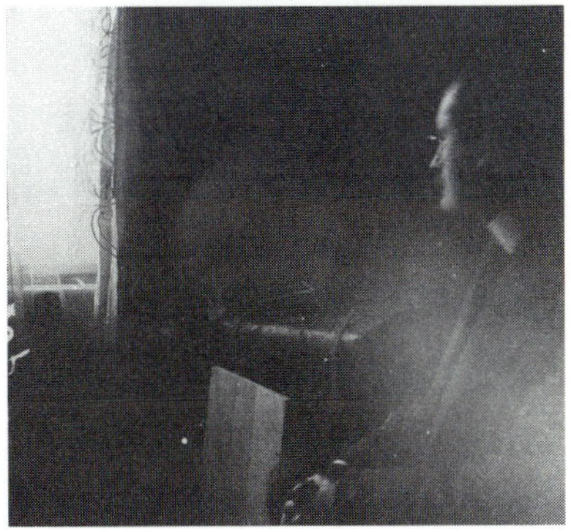

Munch in an unidentified room, probably 1906

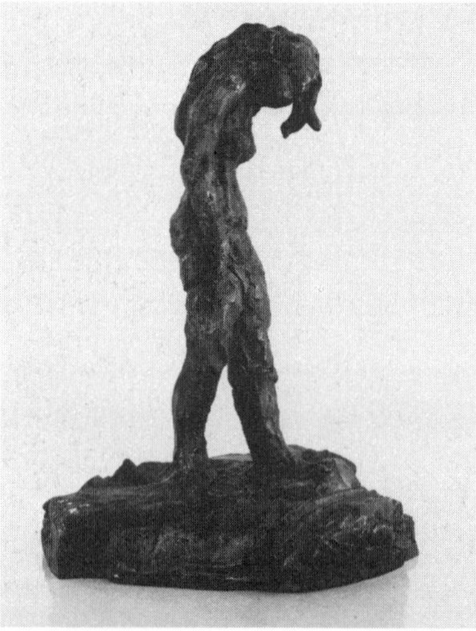

Weeping Girl, 1909-14 Bronze sculpture

To the left another woman can be seen in light-coloured clothes, her right hand in front of her mouth, her left on her hip. The light fog to the left of the woman on the photograph can most easily be explained by her having moved in and out of the field of vision during the exposure, which shows that this effect was intended by Munch. One of the women was most probably Rosa Meissner, a professional model, who Munch had used in Berlin in 1906, and took with him to Warnemünde in August 1907; the other woman is probably her sister Olga who accompanied her. There is a similarity of feature in the faces of the two women, which can give the illusion of the woman looking at herself. The photograph conveys a concentrated atmosphere, filled with presentiment, which makes it a major work in Munch's photographic oeuvre, and is the one photograph of Munch's which gives the strongest association with so-called *spirit photography*.

Already established in the 1880's, *spirit photography* is now an almost forgotten photographic tradition, which both Munch and Strindberg were excited by in their time. It was often a question of showing a medium sitting in a chair; and behind or beside her the deceased appeared as a light, more or less identifiable shape. It was believed that the spirit of the deceased could be *'seen'* by the photographic plate. Strindberg, for instance, had a picture of Paul Verlaine on his deathbed, at which he could see a series of spirit-like figures. Munch had probably been facinated by the phenomenon of *spirit photography* in 1886, when he was working on the painting ***The Sick Child*** and he was obviously interested in the phenomenon in Berlin in 1893. As late as 1907, Munch gave Gustav Schiefler the impression that he saw aura-like shapes around people, and at the time when he took his most experimental photographs in Warnemünde, he was constantly absorbed by similar thoughts, as the following notes prove:

"Are there spirits
We see what we see
because we have eyes that are so made

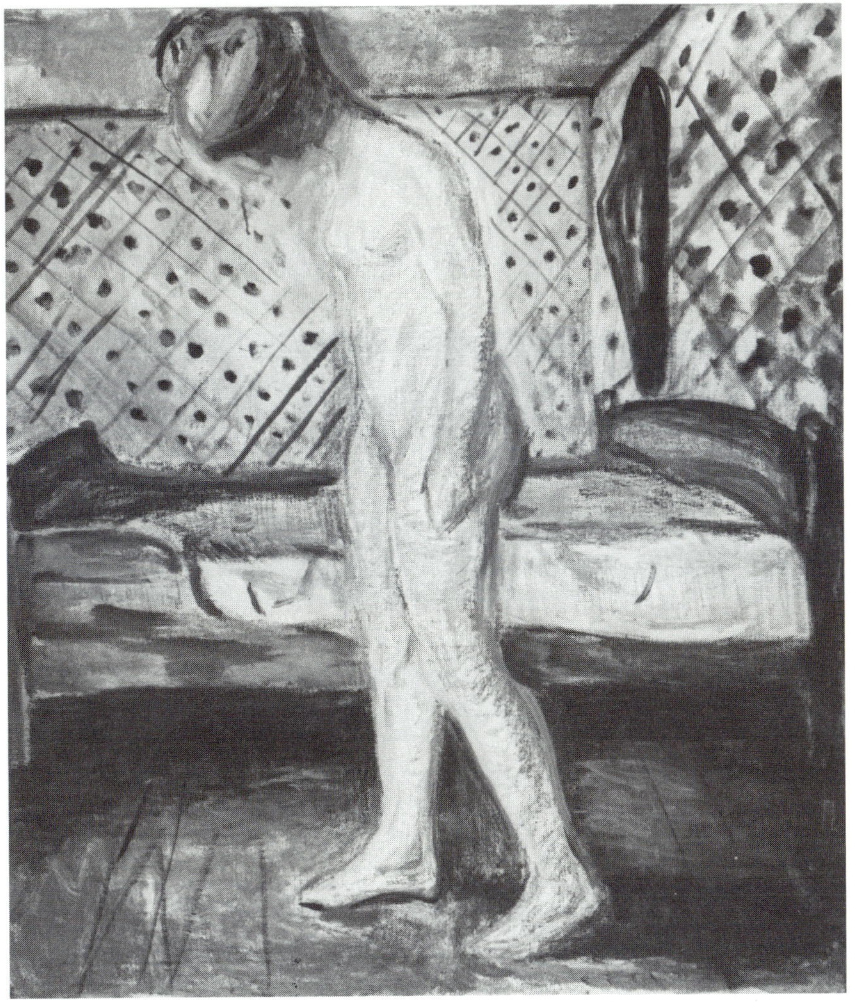

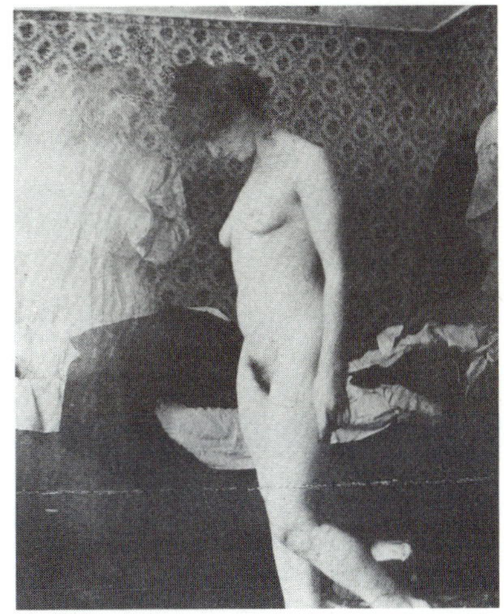

Rosa Meissner at the Hotel Rohne, Warnemünde 1907

Weeping Girl, 1907 Oil on canvas

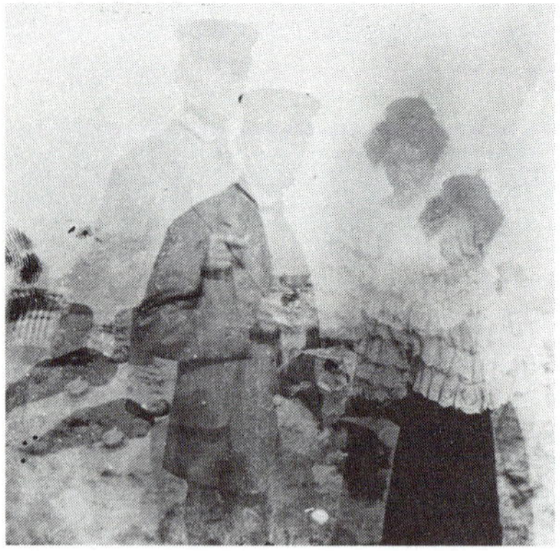

Munch and Rosa Meissner on the beach, Warnemünde 1907

What are we ?

A collection of moving power - a light which burns - with a wick - now the inner heat - now the outer flame - and still an invisible flame-ring -

If our eyes were made differently - we would like X-rays see only our wicks -

The bone system - Were our eyes of a different nature - could we see our outer flame-rings - and see other human beings of other substances.

Why then should not - other beings made of more-easily dissolved molecules be round us and in us -

The souls of the deceased -

Our dear souls - and evil spirits"

We can see the aforementioned model, Rosa Meissner, palely indicated in some photographs of which the subject is the artist and his model, taken on the beach at Warnemünde in the autumn of 1907.

In one of these photographs Munch is standing with his thumb in his trouser pocket and a cigarette in his mouth. He seems to be a strong and healthy man. The model by his side, probably Rosa Meissner, is shy and sweet. Munch's hand is also emphasised here, and we can clearly see the shortened middle finger, but this time it is on his right hand, which shows that the photograph was reversed. Another photograph was taken of the couple, but in a slightly altered position, with either a double exposure or a diagonal movement of the camera during exposure. A double record by the camera gives a '*double vision*' here, which could be a phenomenon of perceptual psychology. Munch was at this time specially interested in the notion of split personality: how one can '*walk side by side with oneself*', a subject which was given expression in paintings like ***The Bricklayer and the Mechanic*** (1908) and the ***Drowned Child*** (1908). The photograph appears almost dreamlike, unreal. Munch copied it both in a correct and reversed version.

One of his most fascinating photographic self-portraits was originally

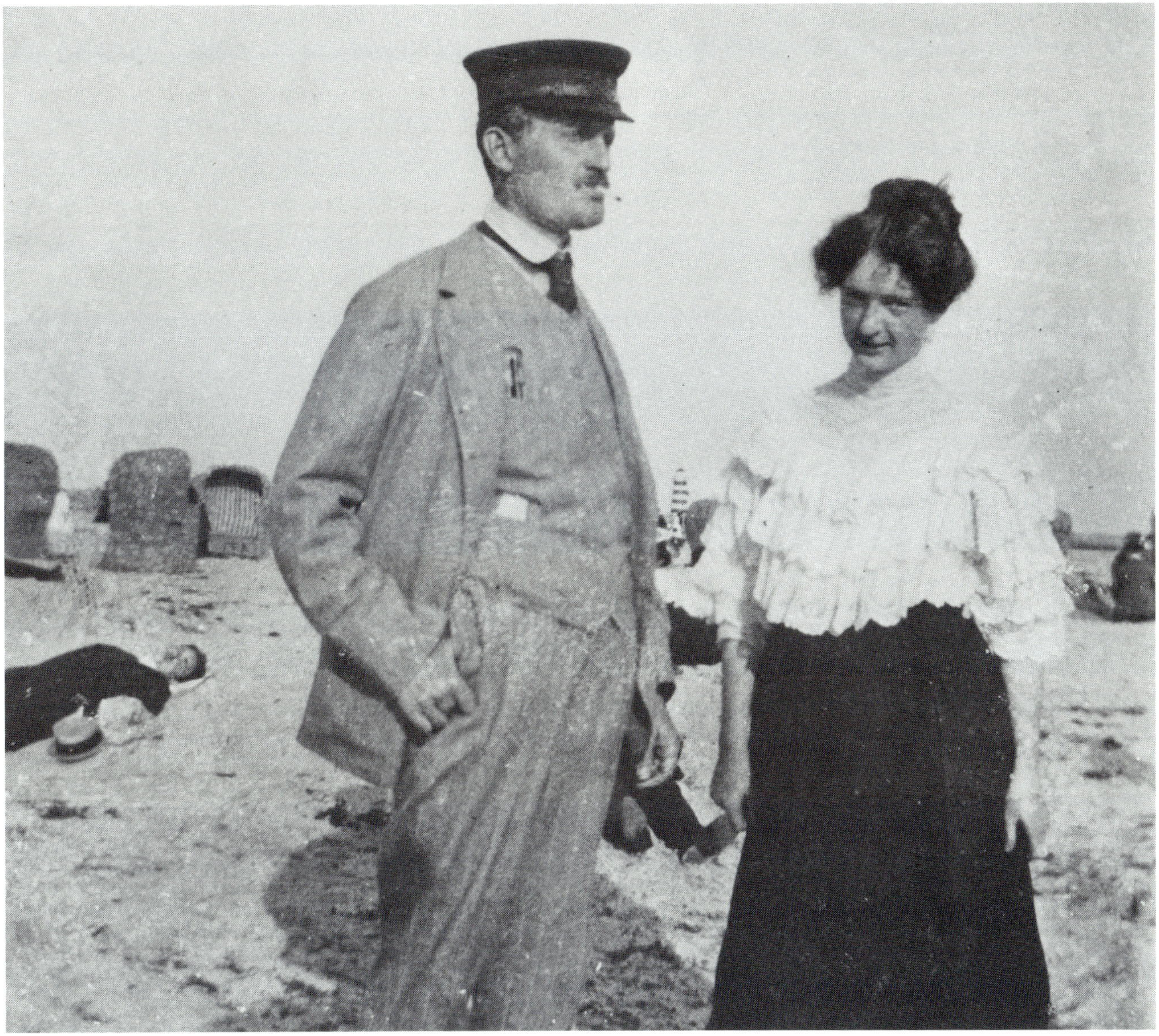

Munch and Rosa Meissner on beach, 1907

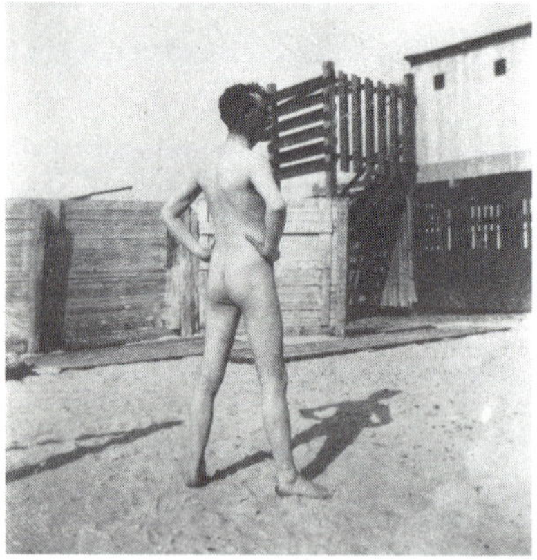

Munch posing at Warnemünde 1907

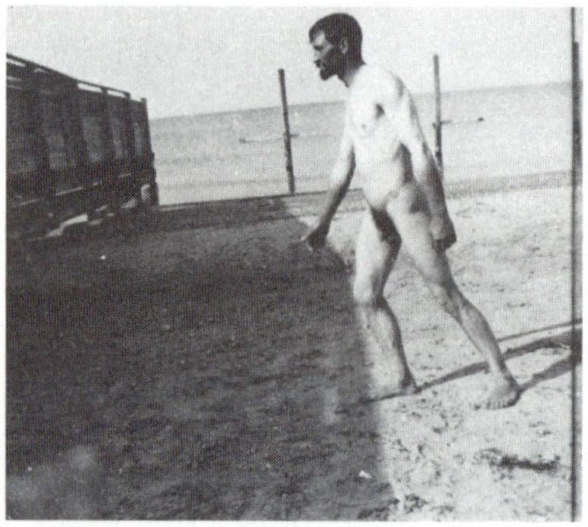

Male model on the beach Warnemünde 1907

taken in Warnemünde in 1907. He is standing at the entrance of Am Strom 53, between the painting of the ***Children in the Street***, a subject from a lane running behind the house, and ***Old Man***, painted in the picturesque back yard. Behind Munch is a recently-begun version of ***The Sick Child***, a commission from his Swedish patron, Ernst Thiel. The photograph has been double exposed so ***The Sick Child*** can be seen dimly through the artist. Munch's right hand is hidden in his trouser pocket. We cannot see his damaged hand either, but judging from the pose it should be approximately at the place where the models of ***The Sick Child***, his late mother and sister, consolingly let their hands meet. Is the fusion consciously related to Munch's own words : *"In the same chair in which I painted the patient, I and all my dear ones - from my mother onwards - have been sitting winter after winter - staring longingly towards the sun- until death called them."?*

The photograph can also be interpreted from another angle: Munch standing in his male virility between childhood and old age, represented by the paintings ***Children in the Street*** (1907) and ***Old Man*** (1907). The same symbolism can be found in the triptych ***Bathing Men*** which was painted in that same summer of 1907, where the side-panels show respectively youth and old age. Munch took a whole series of photographs of himself and his models during his work on that monumental bathing-picture. In the three full-length nude pictures of the artist himself, front and back, the damaged hand is never shown. In the open air it was of no importance. The models he used were bathing attendants attached to the nudist beach where Munch set up his canvas. Having been the scenery and decoration producer at the Kammerspieltheater in Berlin that winter, under the direction of Max Reinhardt, he posed the bathing attendants as if they were on a stage.

After a slight stroke Munch agreed to go into Dr Jacobson's private clinic in Copenhagen about the 1st October 1908; another reason, of course, was to help him deal with his alcohol problem.

After a few days of rest, he turned his room into a studio. The last of

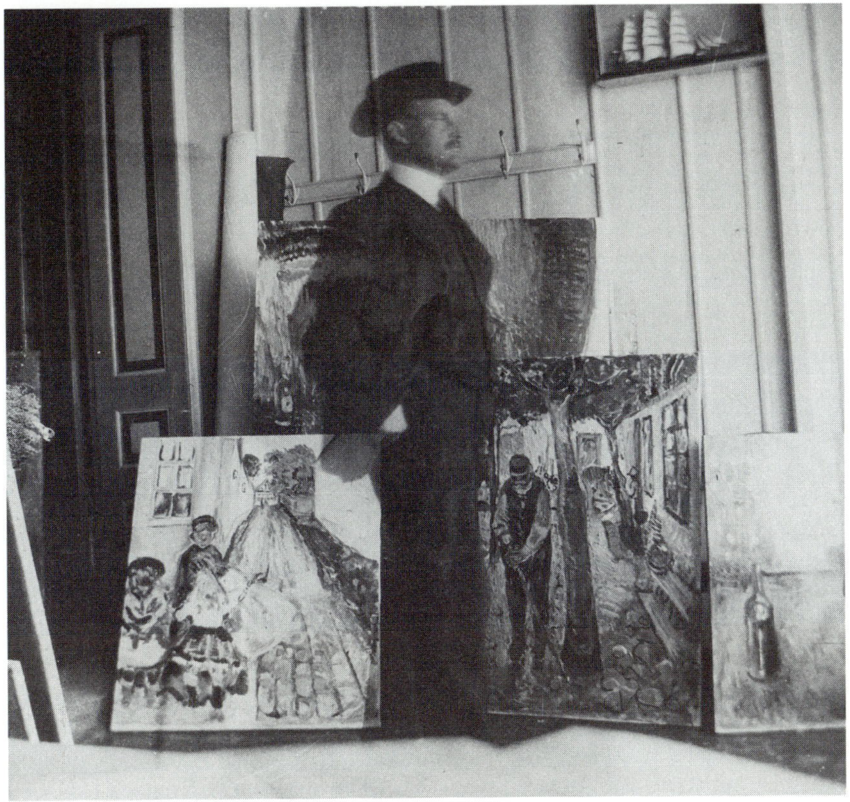

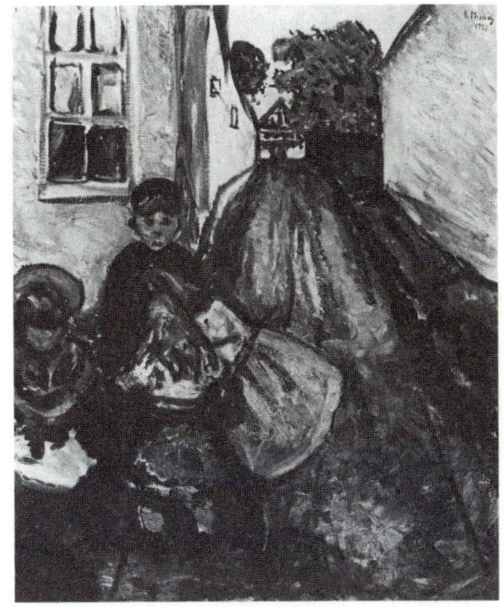

Children in the Street, Warnemünde, 1907 Oil on canvas

Munch in the hall of Am Strom 53, Warnemünde, 1907

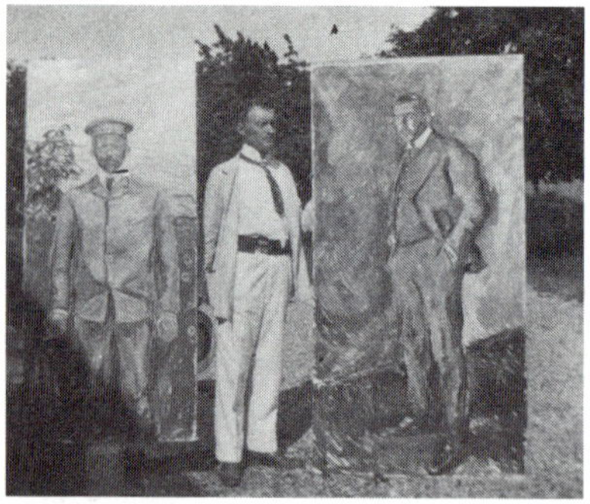

Munch with portraits of Ravensberg and Nilssen, 1909-10

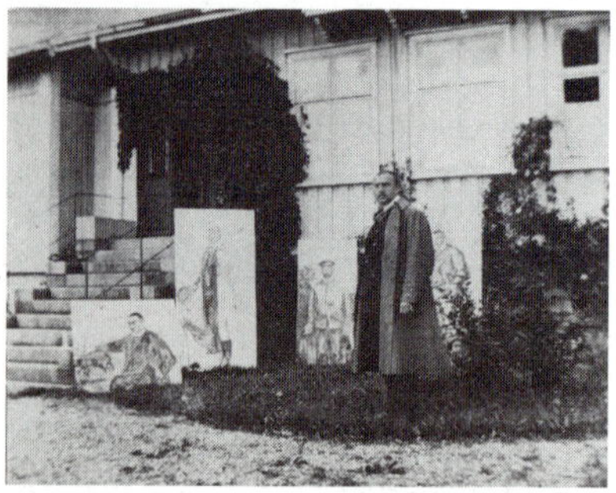

Christian Gierloff, Kragerø 1909-10

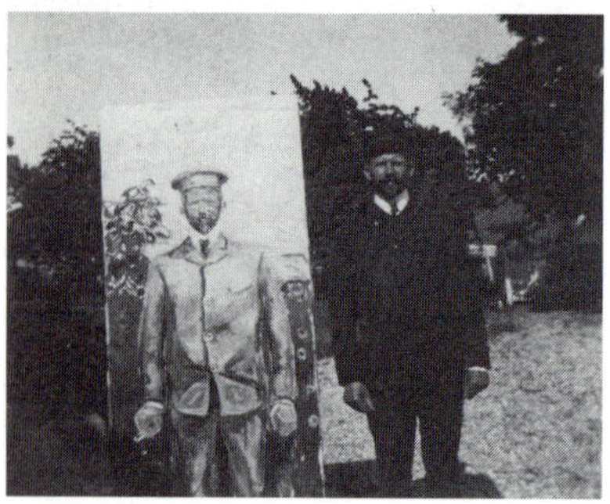

Ravensberg and portrait, 1909-10

the photographs from what Munch called his *Destiny Photograph* period were taken there.

In one of these photographs Munch can be seen sitting with a cigarette in his right hand, whilst his damaged hand is resting on the arm of a chair. He is sitting opposite the newly-started painting ***Self-Portrait from the Clinic***, where the right hand is conspicuous and symbolically charged; Munch looks at himself in the self-portrait as if it were a mirror. Between the artist and the portrait , however, a smiling nurse can be seen bringing in some food. The tension is dissolved.

The rest of Munch's photographs from this period in Copenhagen seem to be more humorous, even self-parodying, as for instance an exaggeratedly foreshortened picture of himself in a bathroom. This is a paraphrase of one of his favourite subjects, the ***Death of Marat***, which was motivated by the shooting incident at Åsgårdstrand in September 1902.

After travelling along the south coast of Norway in the spring of 1909, Munch decided to rent the property Skrubben near Kragerø with its impressive view over the sea and the many islands. Here he collected ideas both for a series of landscapes and the mural in the University Hall in Oslo.

A series of photographs, taken with Munch's camera, shows him and his friends Jappe Nilssen, Christian Gierløff and Ludvig Ravensberg beside their respective portraits which Munch painted that summer. The photographs were taken at a time when the portraits were more or less finished, with the models posing beside the painting in imitation of the way in which they are depicted in it.

At Skrubben Munch photographed his first sketches for the University murals, at the big outdoor studio which he had had built there. He also took photographs of himself working on a sculpture: a maquette, according to him, for a national monument.

It was not until 1926 that Munch took up photography again. The first pictures he took then mainly record his own works of art. They clearly give

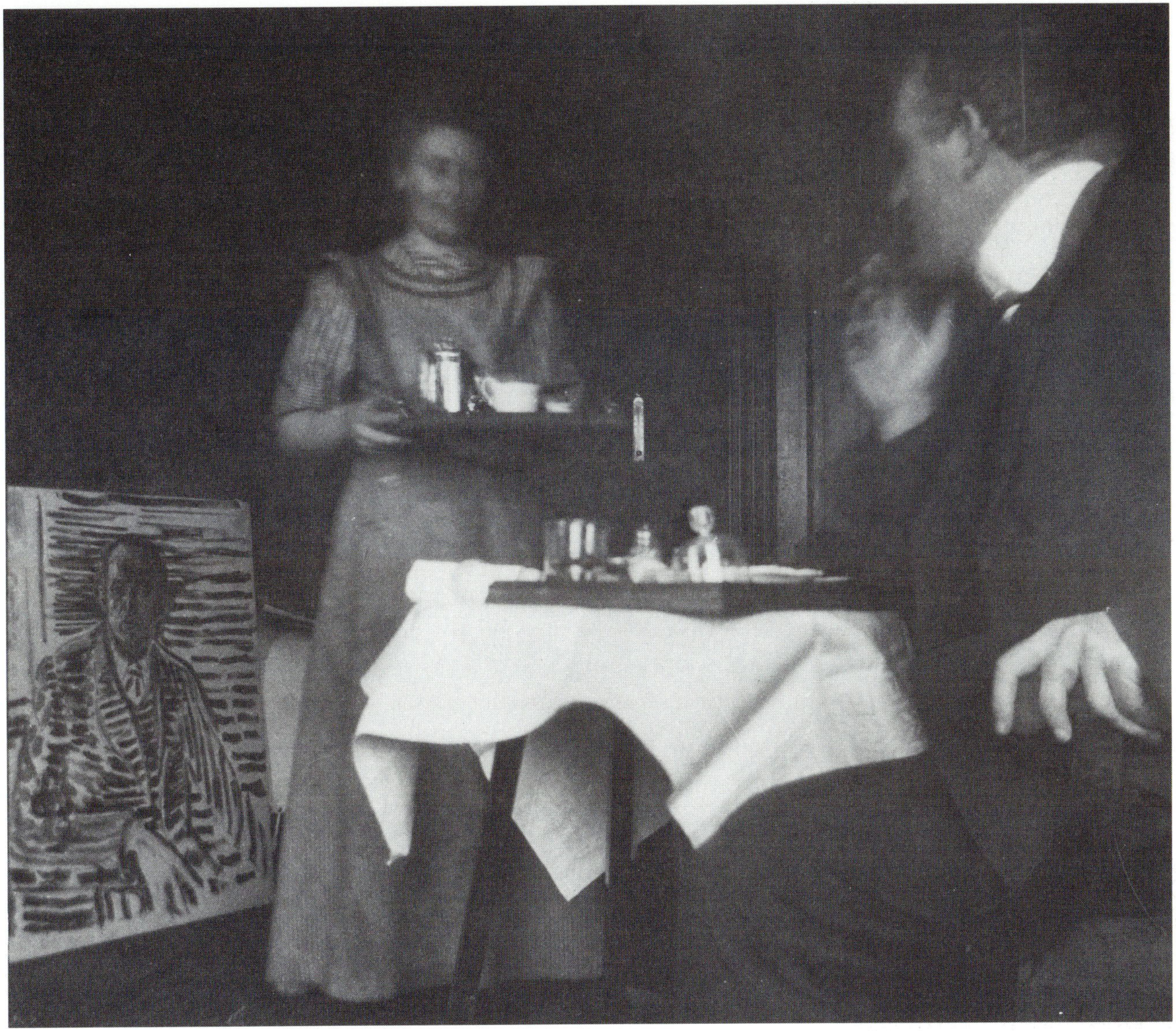

Munch at the breakfast table, the clinic in Copenhagen 1908-09

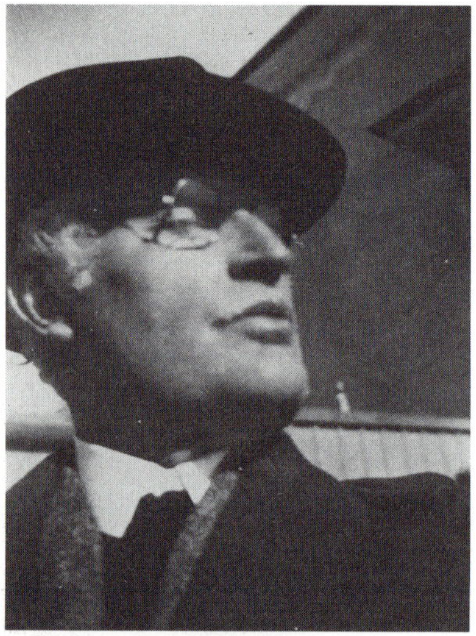

Munch in front of winter studio, Ekely 1930

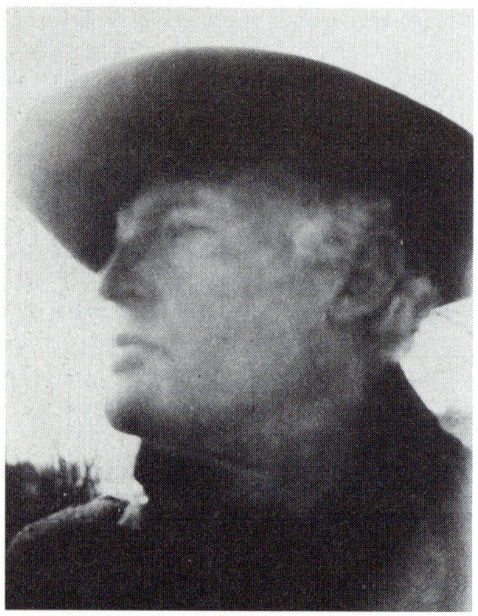

Munch with hat, Ekely 1930

the impression of the camera being tested, and betray no sign of any conscious artistic intent. It seems as if he quite simply wanted to get back into practice.

Quite unexpectedly, a small movie-camera (a so-called Pathe-Baby with a 9.5 mm film-cassette and a projector in a specially-made travel case) was handed in to the Munch Museum a few years ago. This advanced amateur camera was proved to be Munch's by the four films which came with it, all from the summer of 1927. One of the films was taken in Dresden, the other three in Oslo and Aker. The camera has captured trams, cars and horse-drawn carriages, going in all directions. It lingers on crowds of people who are moving past in the street, particularly a man and his wife who are pulling a cart with some difficulty. There is also a row of self-portraits taken outside the conservatory at Ekely.

A vein in his right eye ruptured in May 1930, and caused a considerable reduction in his sight. This was rather serious as the sight in his left eye was already poor. Munch continually monitored the improvement in his condition by drawing the disturbances on his retina during his convalescence. This interest in the mechanics of the eye evidently renewed his interest in Strindberg's ponderings about the inner eye and the optics of photography, and he obtained another camera. He seems consciously to have repeated, with some variations, his *Destiny Pictures* from 1902-1908 but with the difference that it was his own face, with the damaged eye which he tried to pin-point. Most of the photographs are self-portraits taken with the camera at arm's length. His own face appears almost blurred, out of focus, while the paintings in the background are clear and sharp. In the first photographs, his almost abstract watercolours can be seen, with subjects drawn from the disturbances to his sight. In the following years almost crude paintings with sparkling colours, both in oils and watercolours, are evident. In one of the later photographs he appears almost translucent with his latest works of art, painted after his eye trouble, showing through him. Whilst such

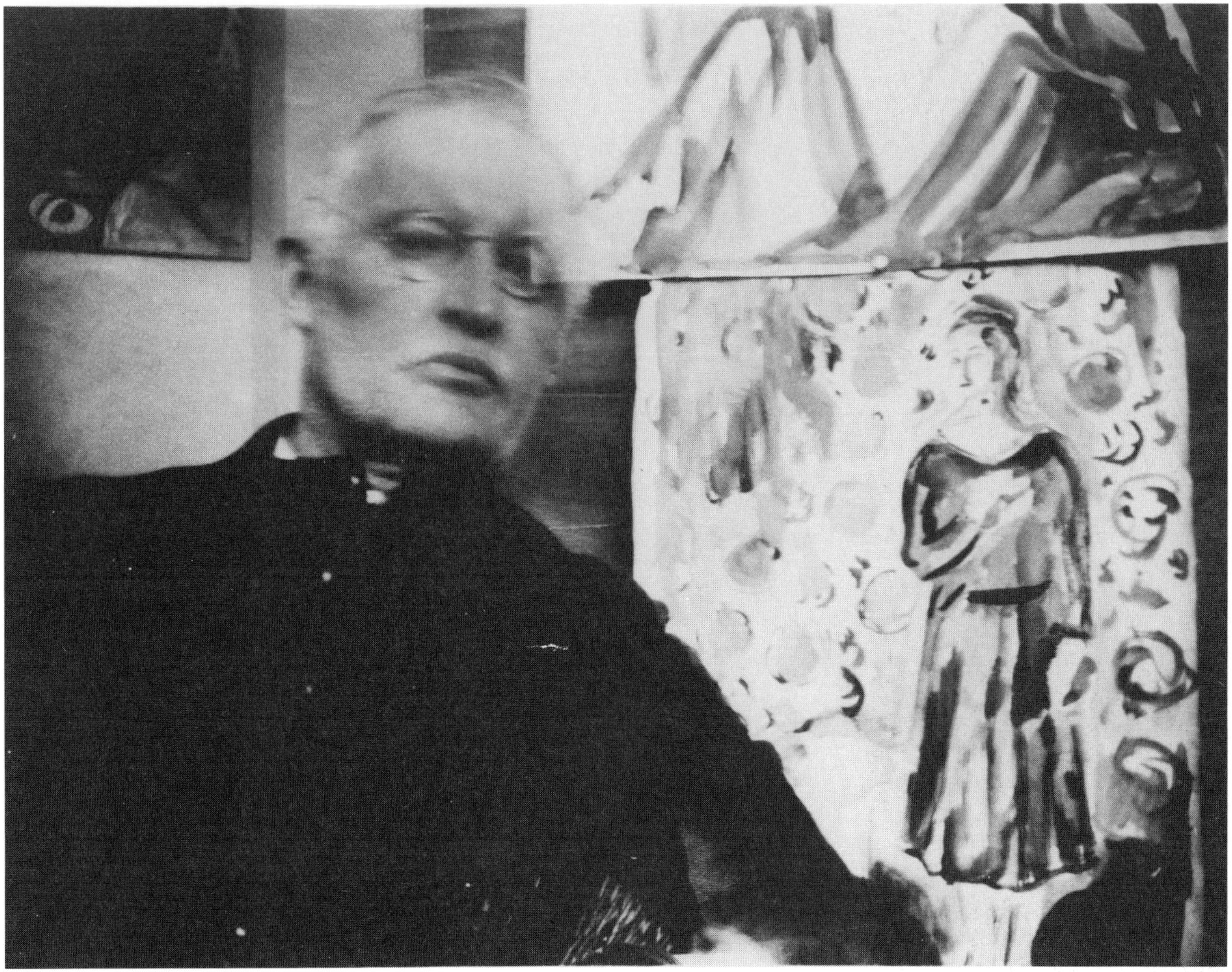

Munch in front of 'Young Girl with Dog' I Ekely 1930

Munch in front of 'Death of Marat' I, Ekely 1930

Munch in front of 'Death of Marat' III 1930

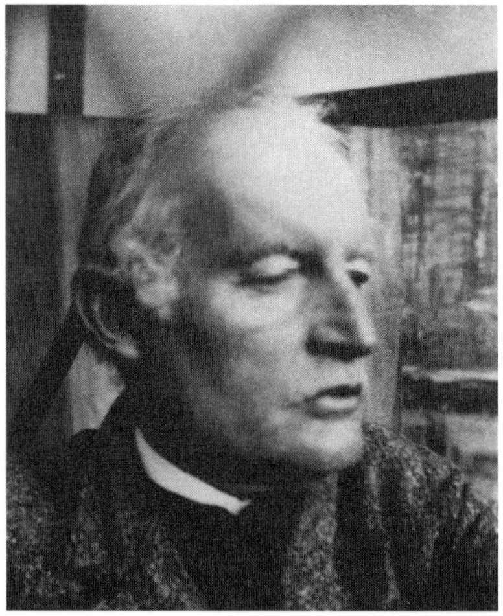

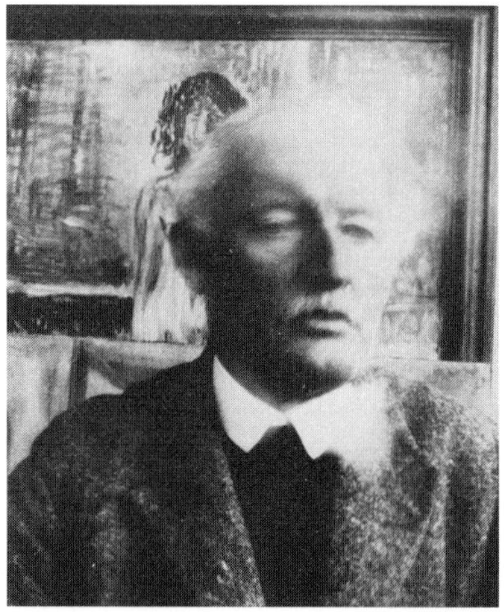

Munch in front of 'Death of Marat' IV 1930

Munch on the veranda at Ekely 1930

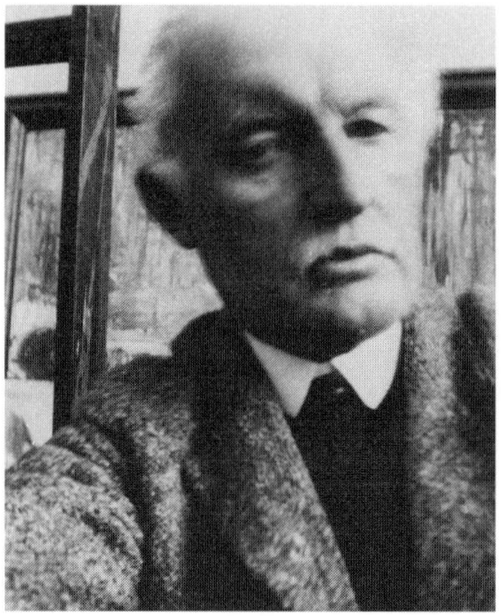

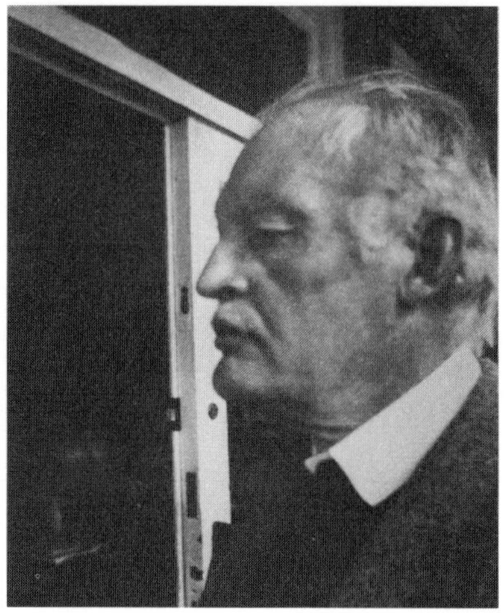

effects in the earlier *Destiny Photographs* acted as a mediator for the artistic experience of melancholy and alienation, he now seems to want to demonstrate the high degree to which he wants to identify with his own artistic production. With support from notes from the winter of 1888 - 1889, it is reasonable to think that Munch originally tried to define the specific and the expressive in his art - *"An art which touches and grips one's own heart's blood"*- in contrast to a photographically-accentuated realism.

When in a couple of small publications in 1929 Munch wanted to retrospectively explain the basic qualifications for his art, he reiterated the following aphorism made in Berlin in about 1904: *"The camera cannot compete with painting as long as it cannot be used in heaven or hell."* The article shows, however, that Munch experimented precisely with expressing and portraying a state of mind, beyond prosaic everyday existence and that he tried to substantiate another dimension in his life: his own hell.

Arne Eggum

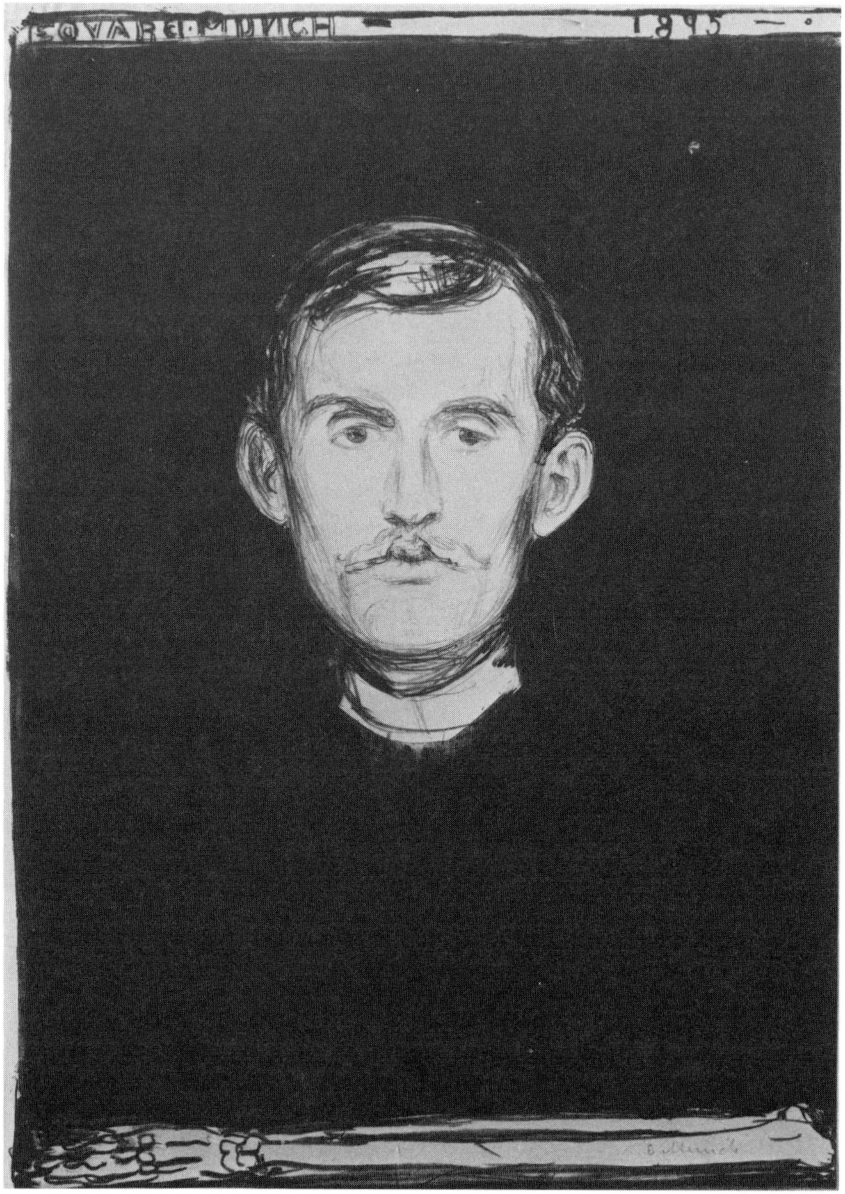

Self-portrait with Skeleton Arm, 1895 Lithograph

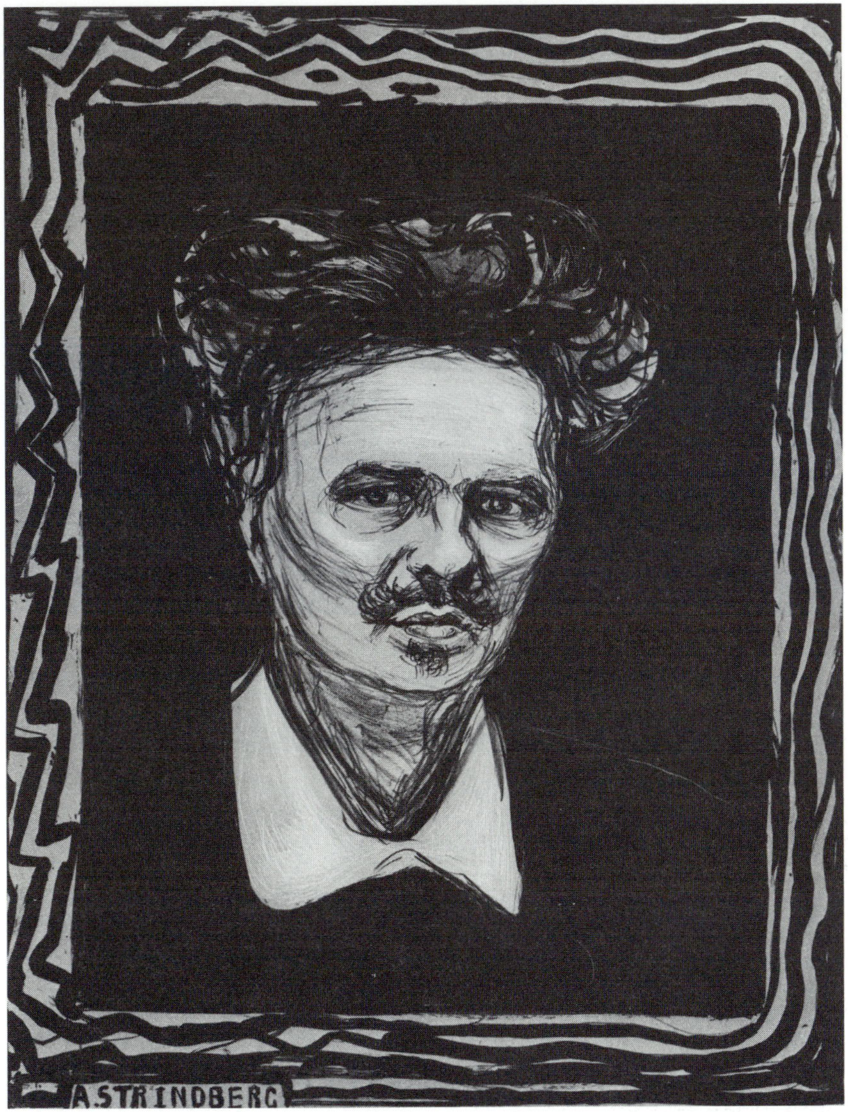

August Strindberg, 1896
Lithograph

In Man's Brain, 1897 Colour Woodcut

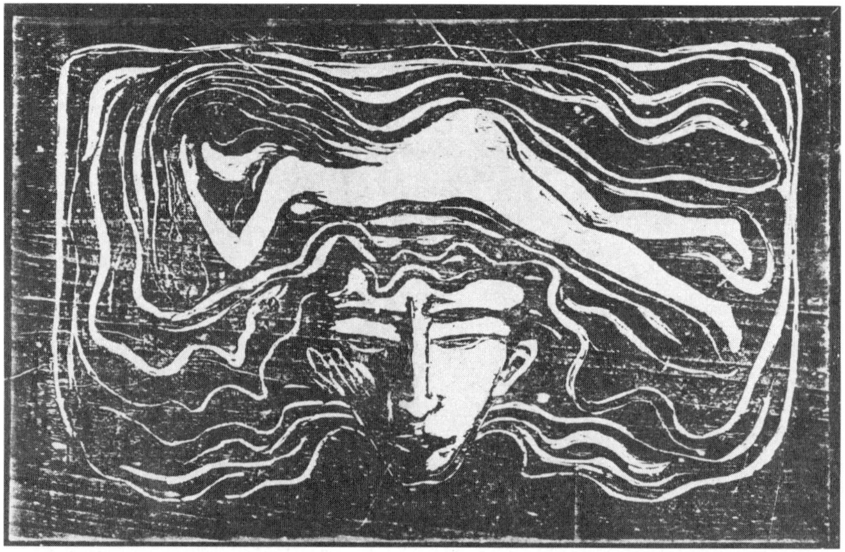

Man's Head in Woman's Hair, 1897 Lithograph

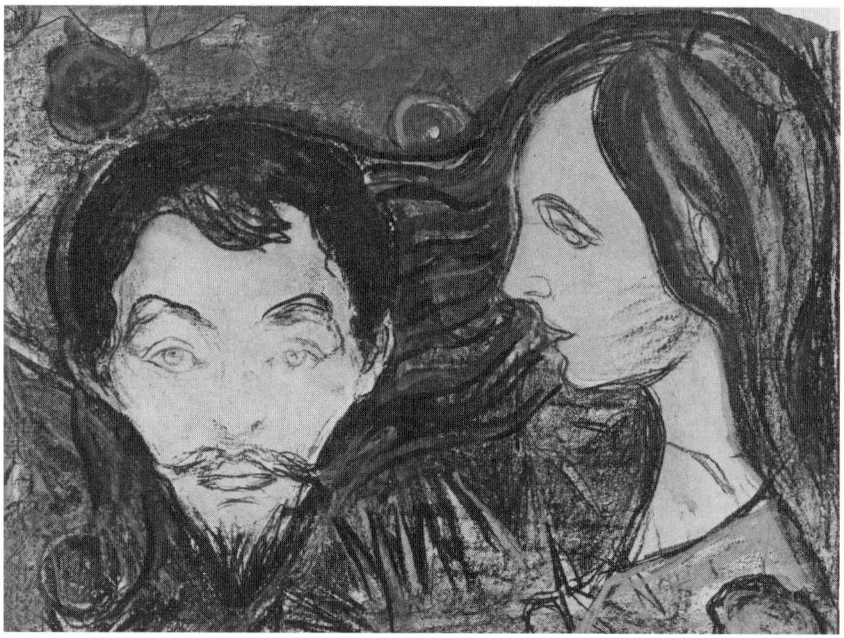

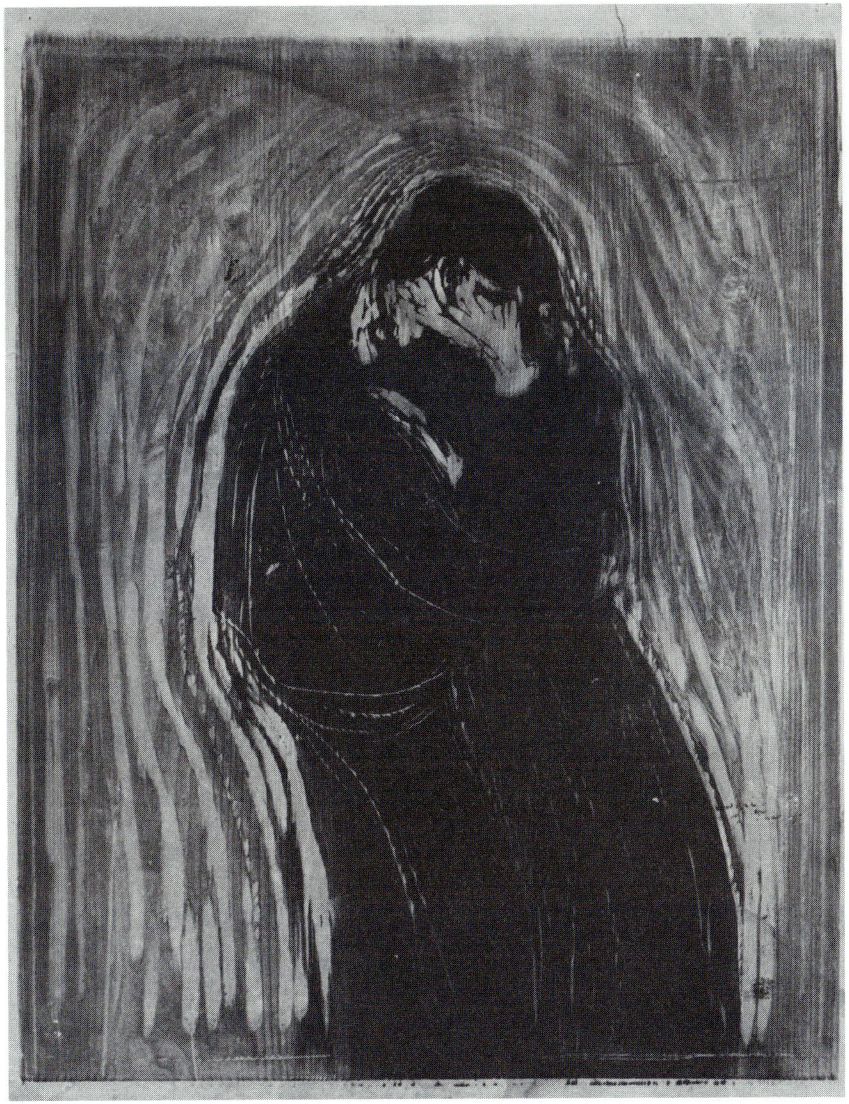

The Kiss, 1897-98 Colour Woodcut

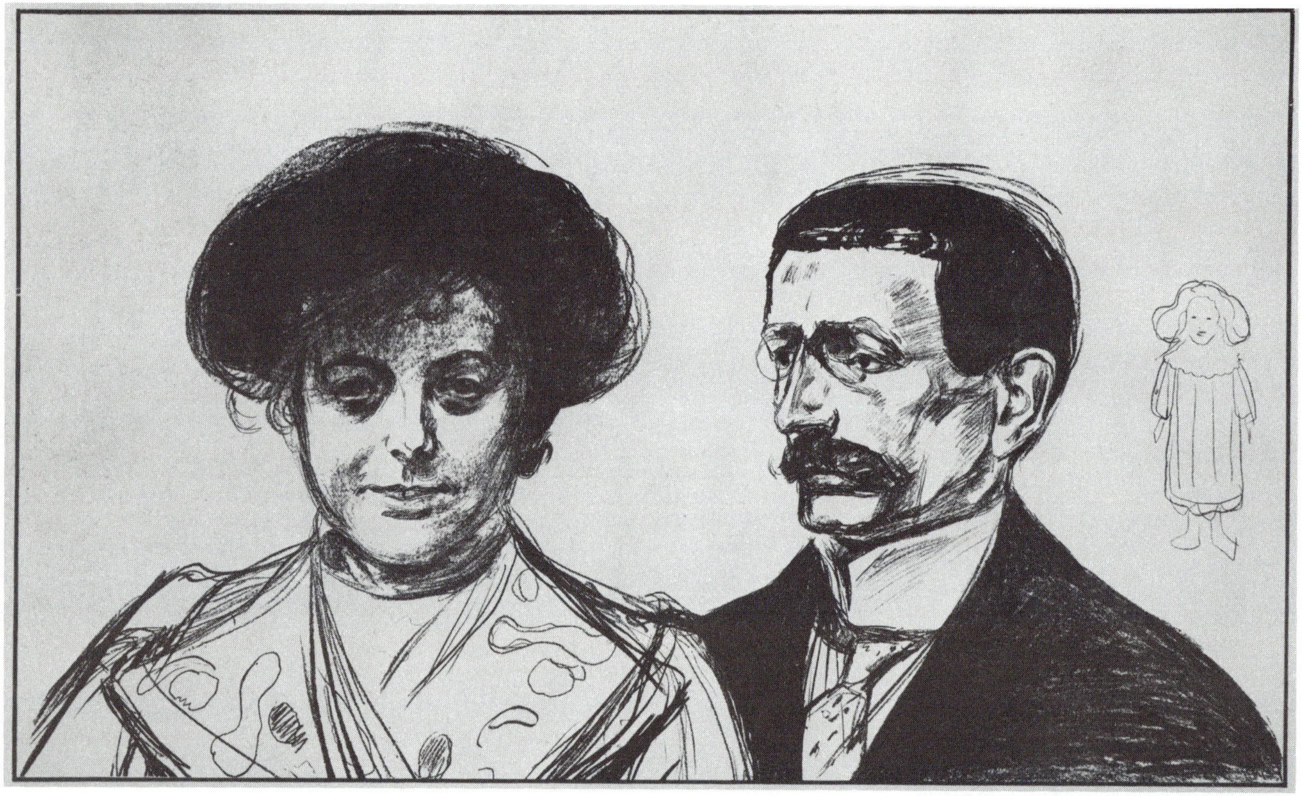

Anna and Walter Leistikow,
1902 Lithograph

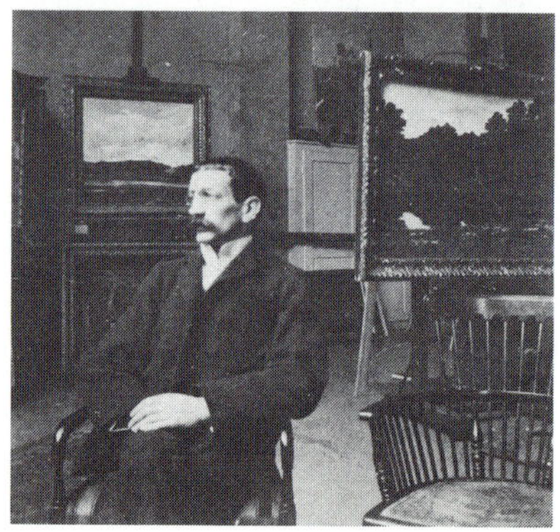

Walter Leistikow in his studio,
Berlin 1902

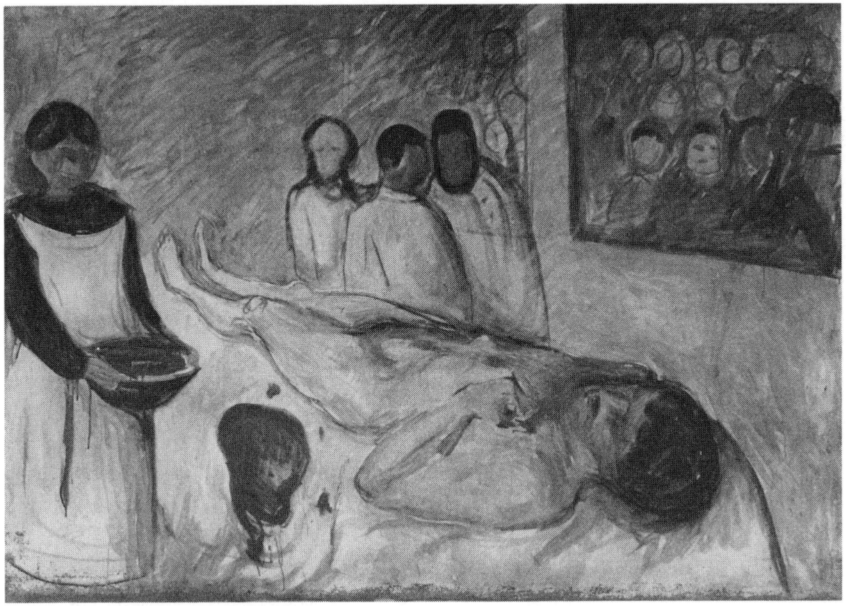

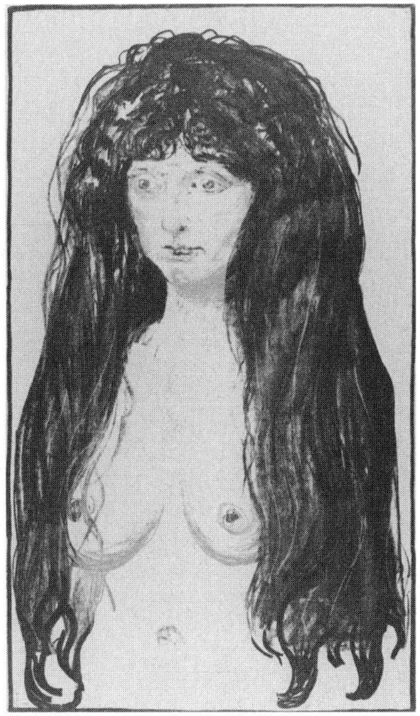

The Sin, 1902 Colour Lithograph

The Operation, 1902 Oil on canvas

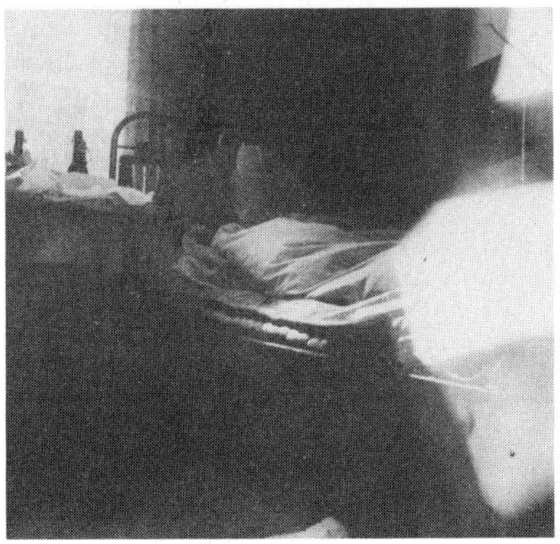

Munch in bed, probably 1902

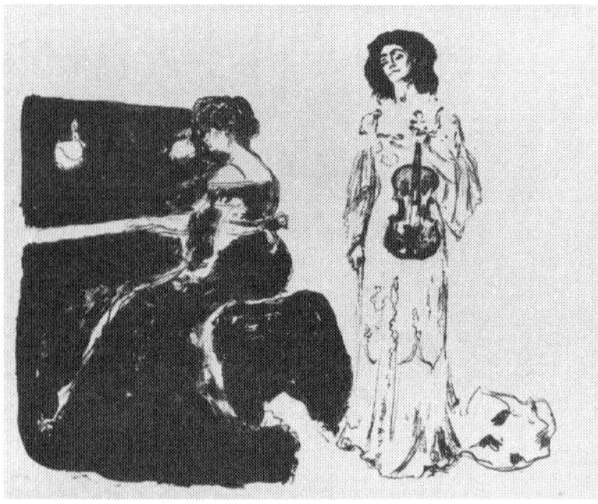

The Violin Concert, 1903
Lithograph

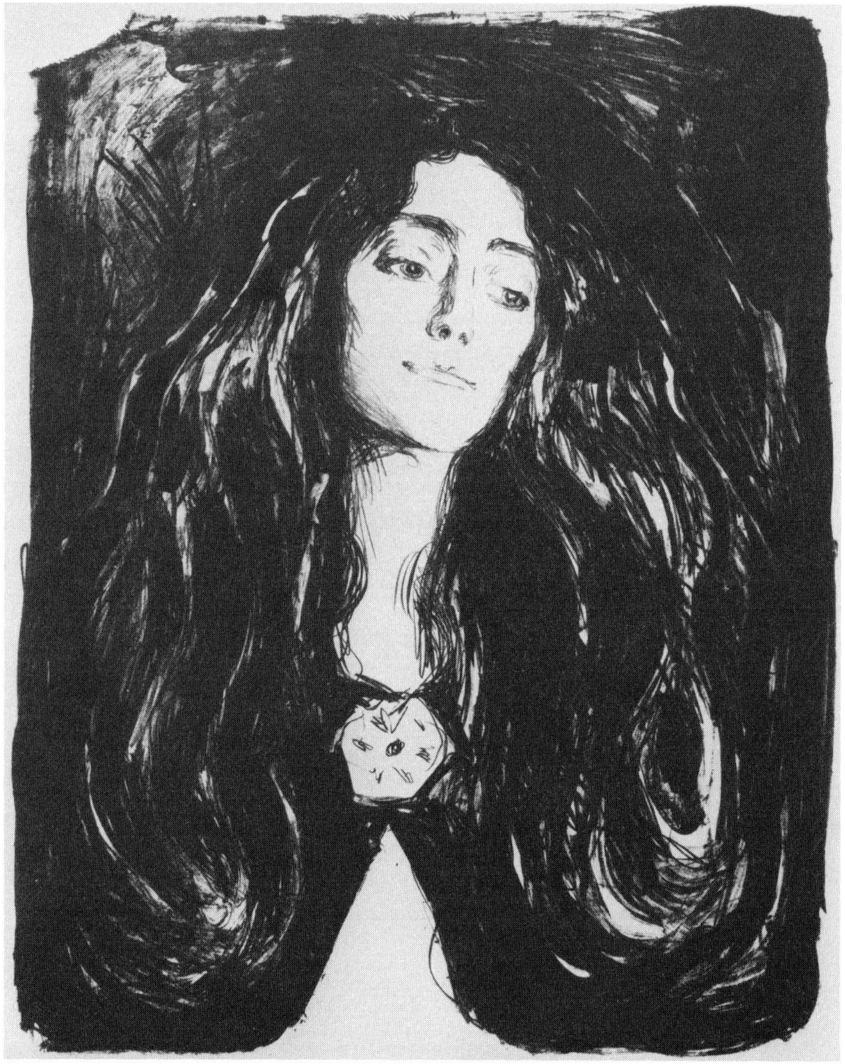

The Brooch: Eva Mudocci 1903
Lithograph

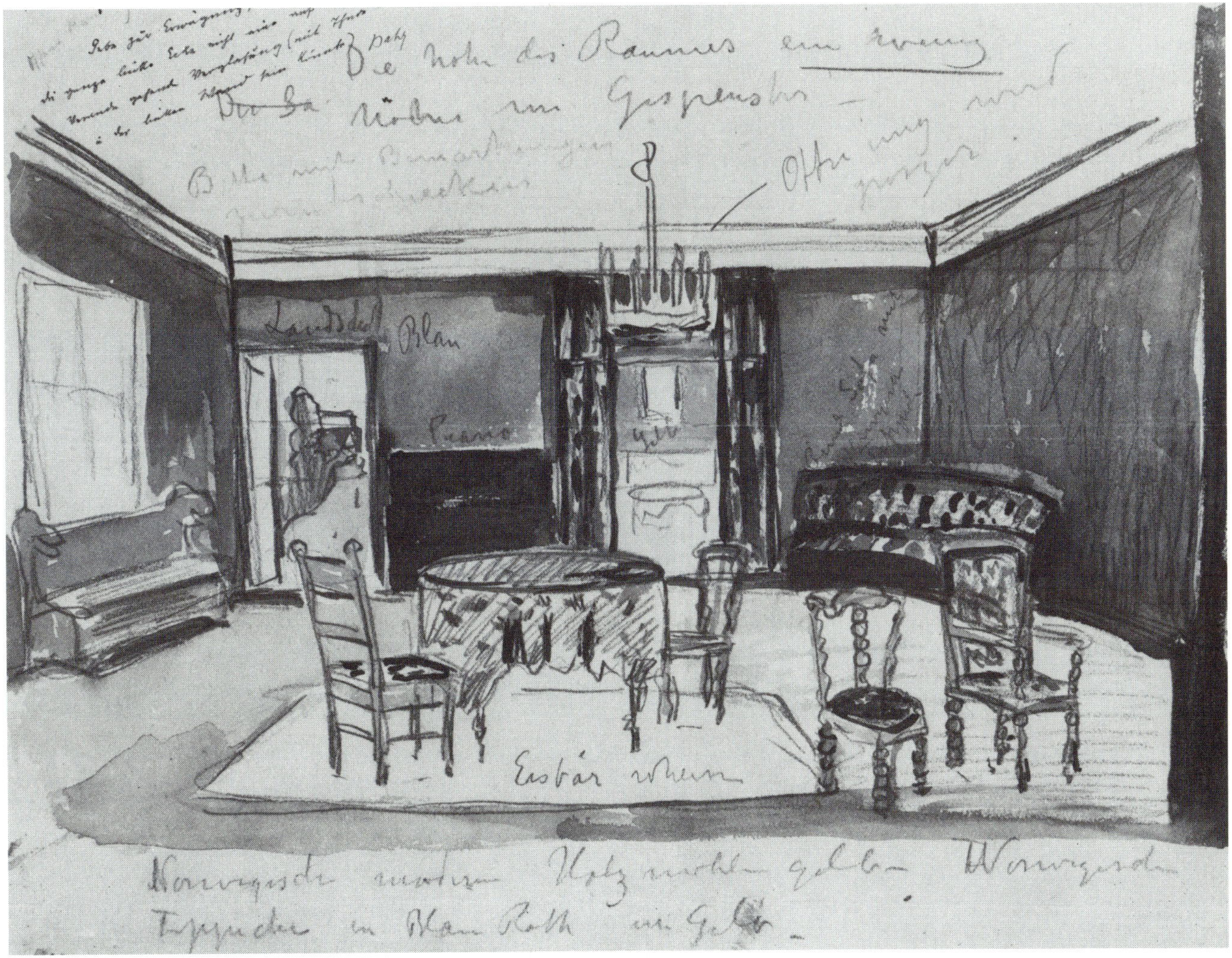

Set for 'Hedda Gabler', 1906
Pencil, crayon, and watercolour

Friedrich Nietzche,
1906-07 Coloured crayon and charcoal on paper

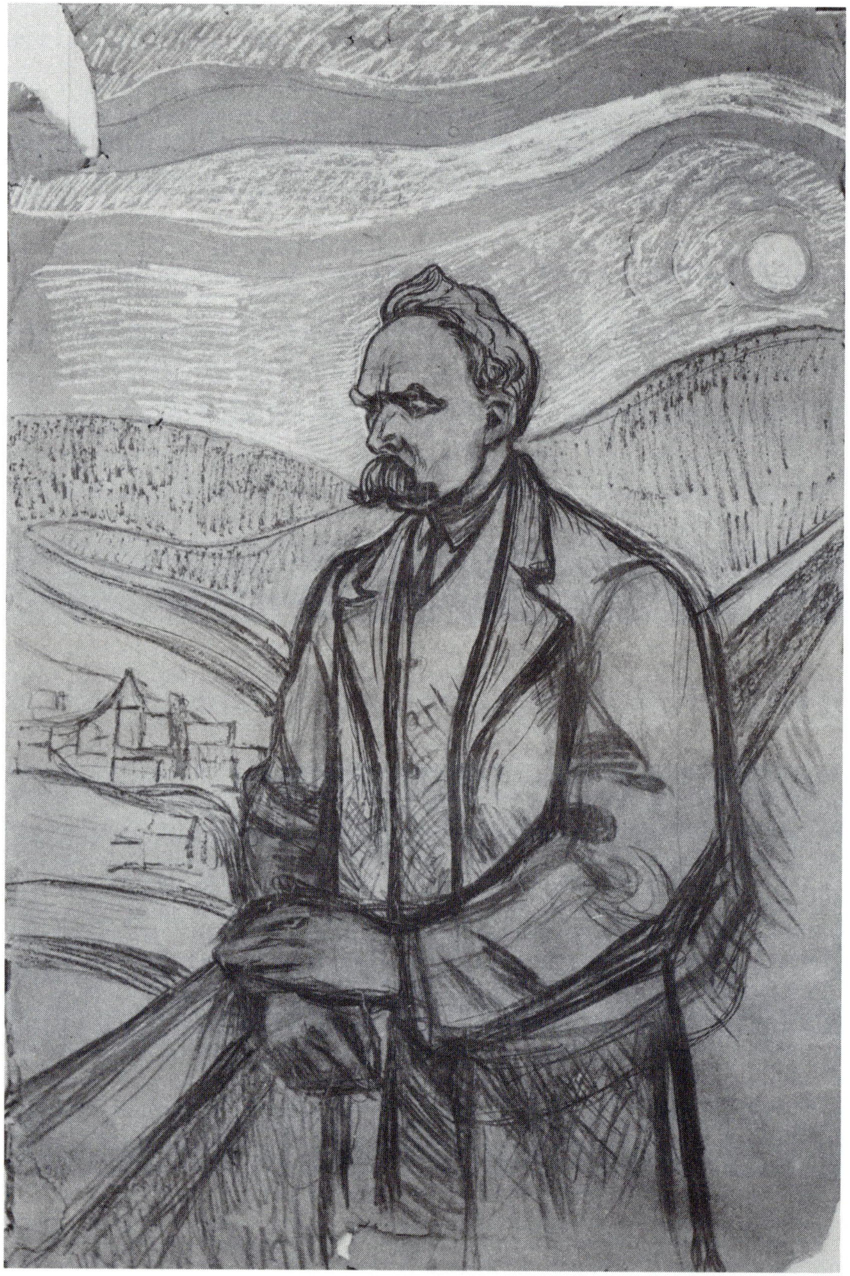

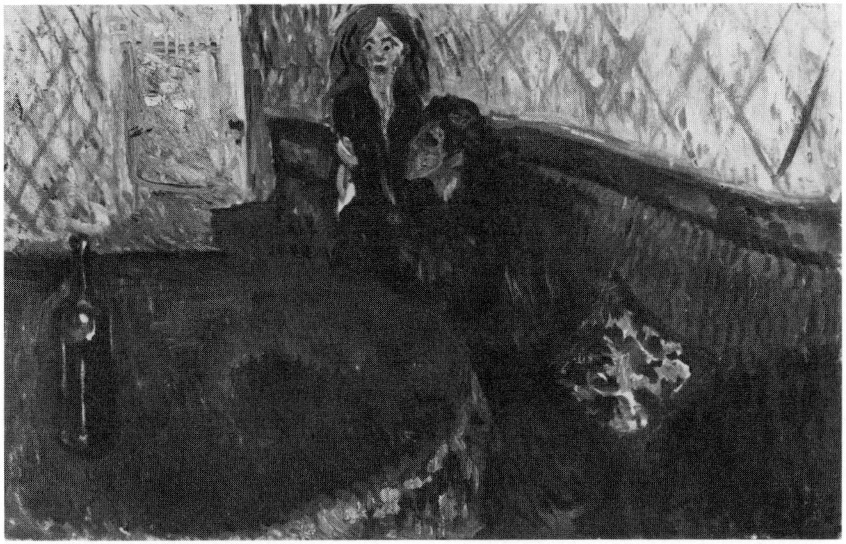

Desire, 1907 Oil on canvas

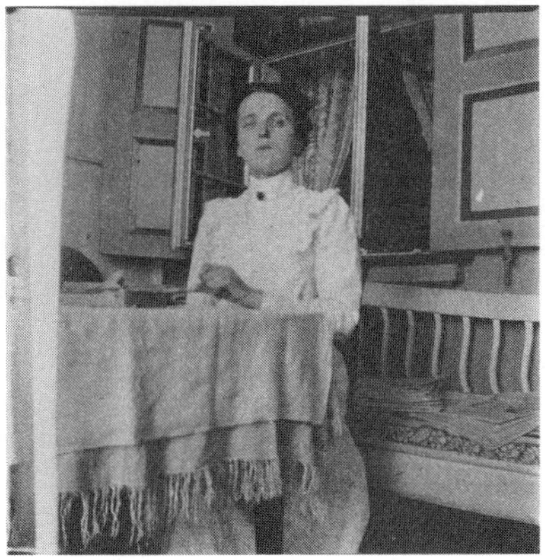

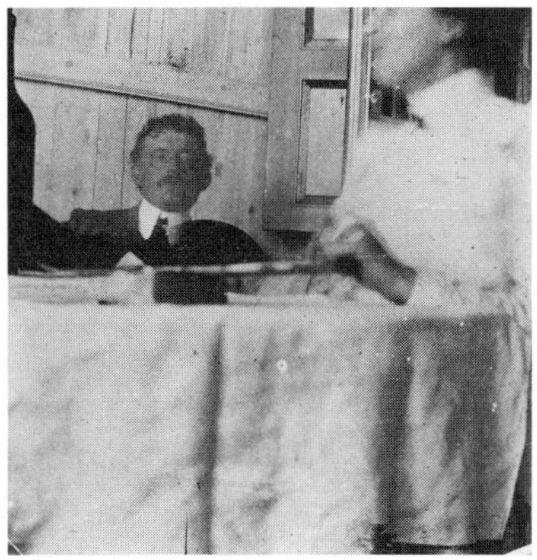

Munch's housekeeper at Am Strom 53, Warnemünde 1907

Munch and housekeeper at Am Strom 53, Warnemünde 1907

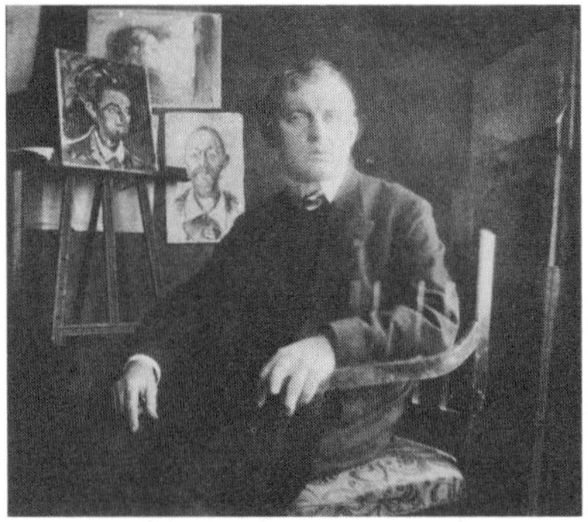

Munch at Dr Jacobson's clinic in Copenhagen 1908-09

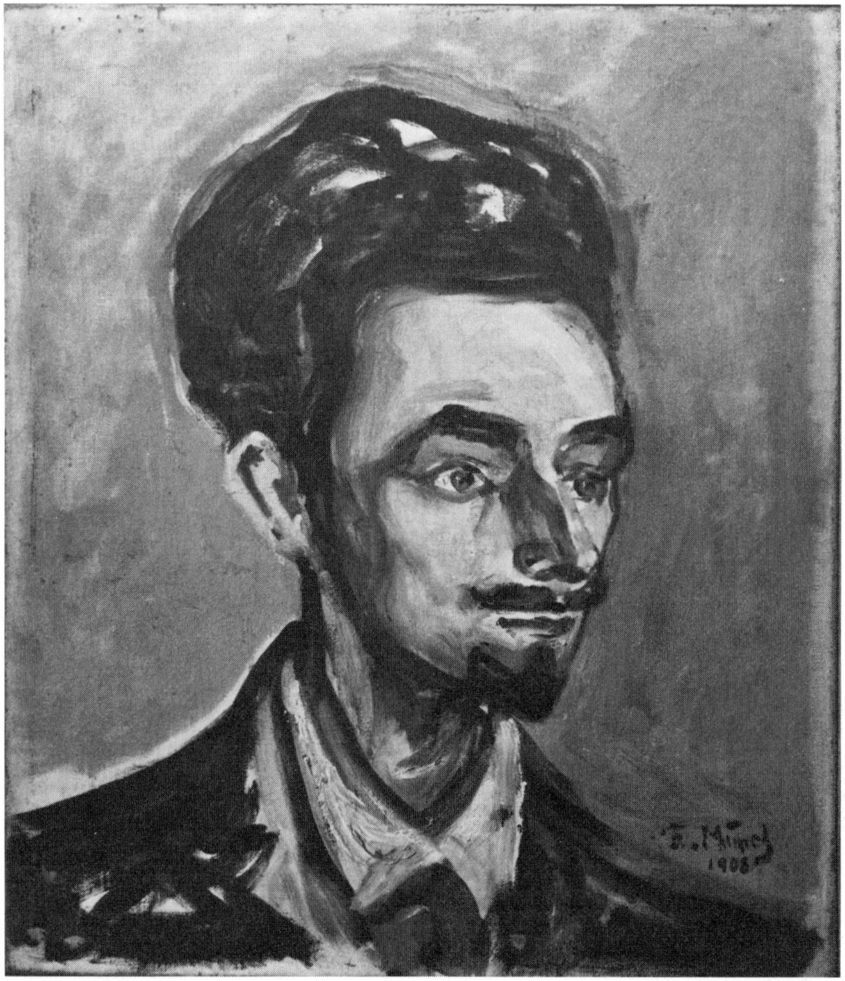

Helge Rode, 1908 Oil on canvas

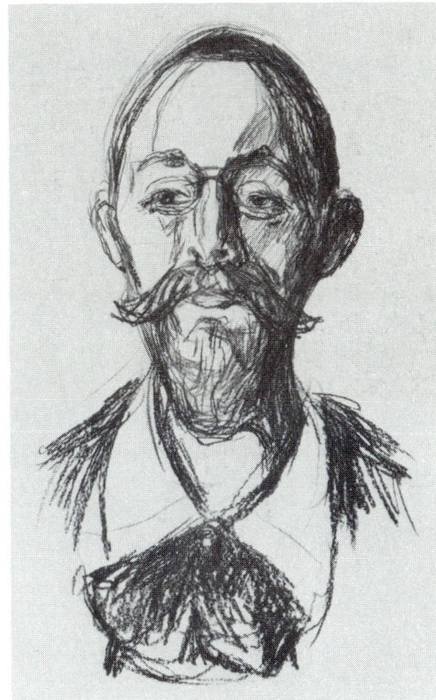

Dr Daniel Jacobson, 1908-09
Lithograph

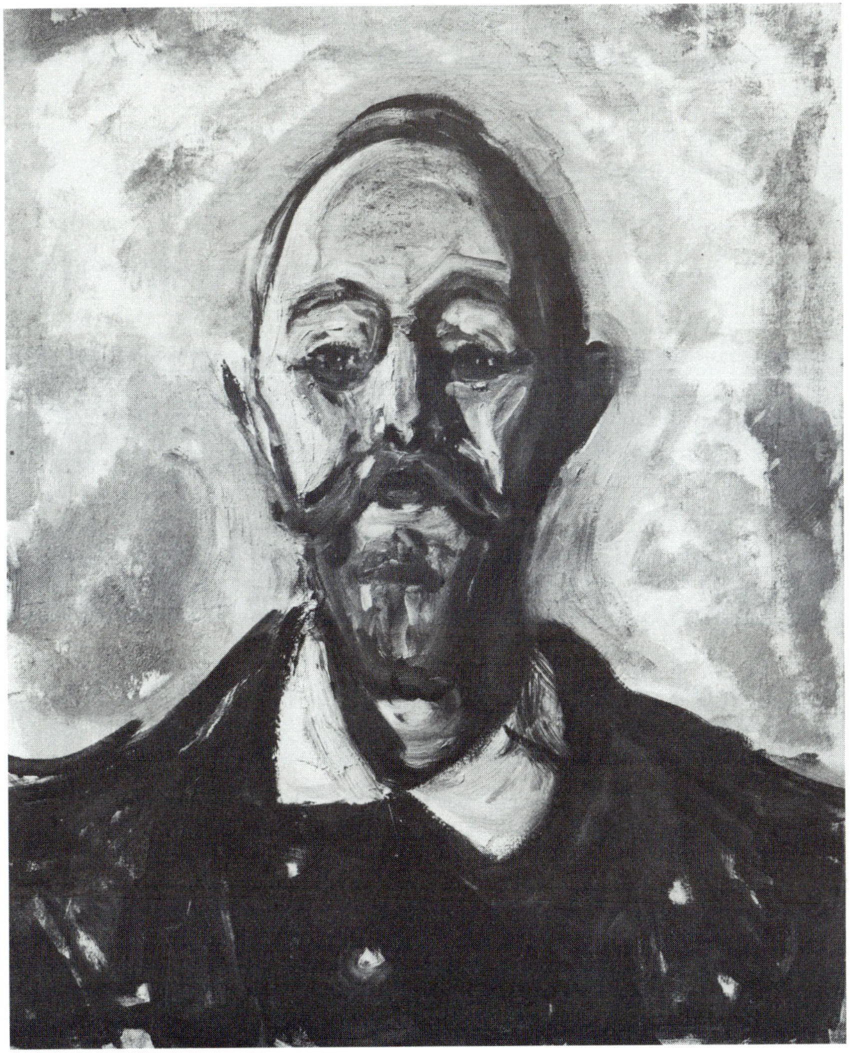

Dr Daniel Jacobson, 1909 Oil on canvas

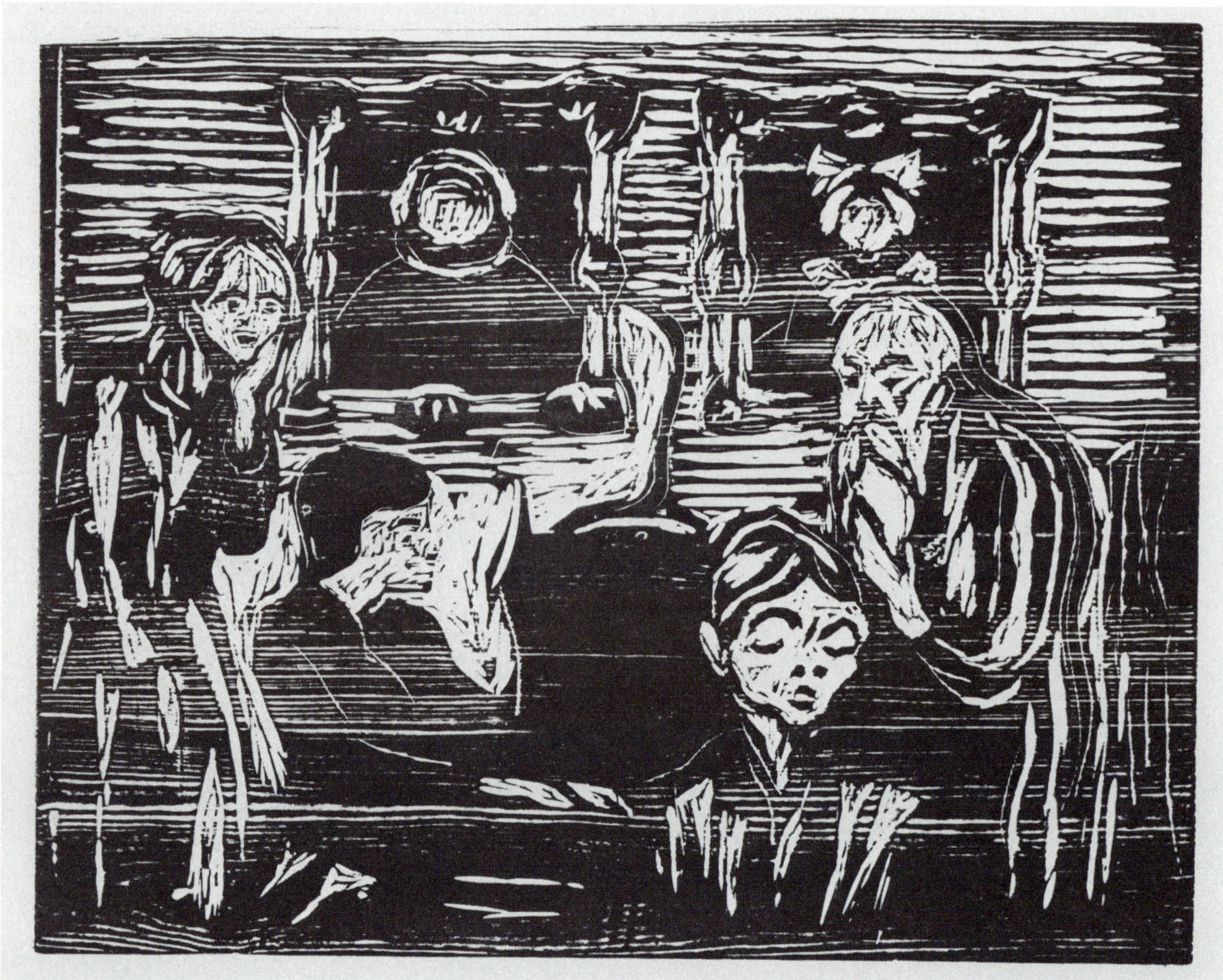

The Son, 1920 Woodcut

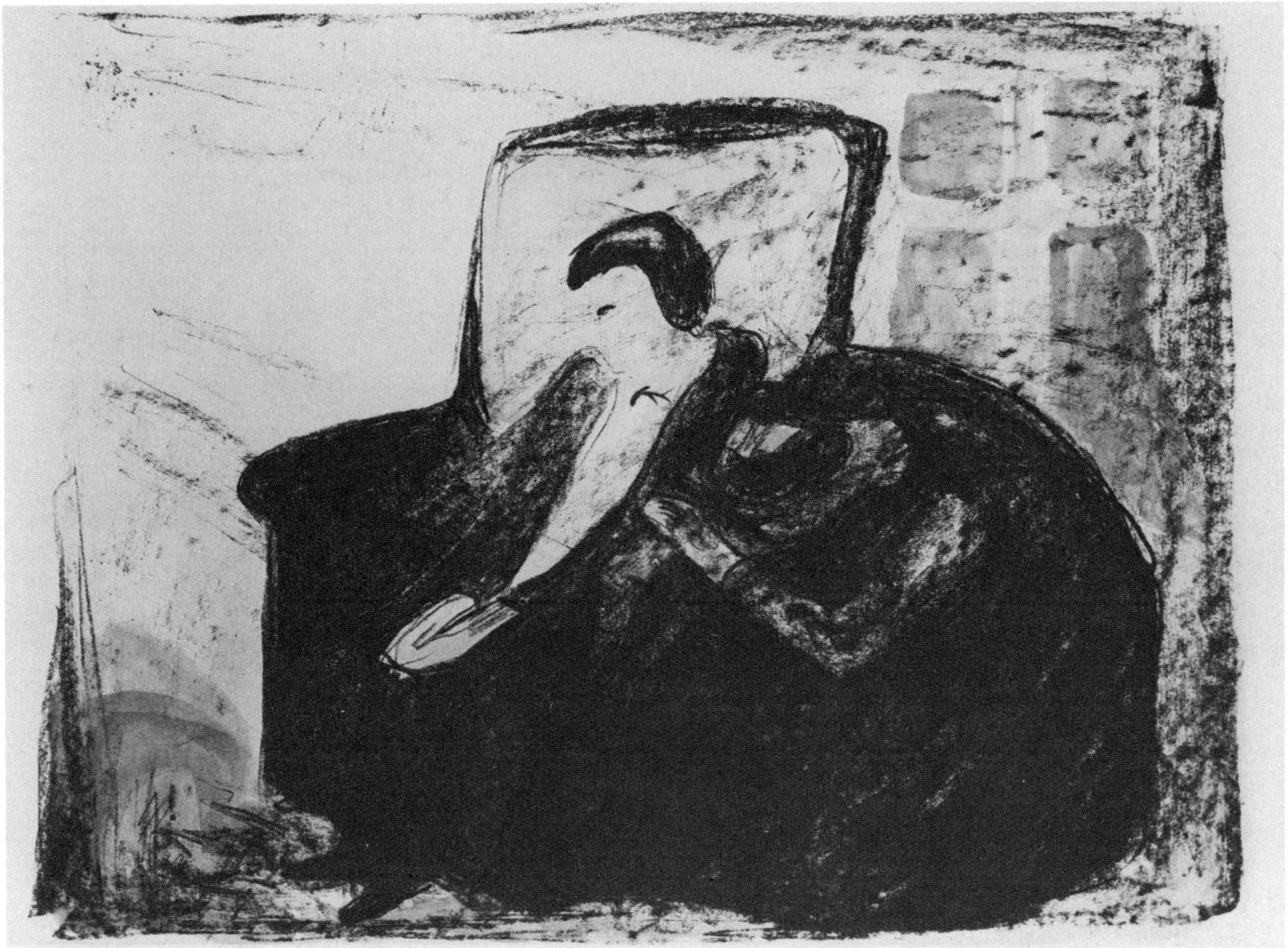

Osvald, 1920 Lithograph, hand-coloured

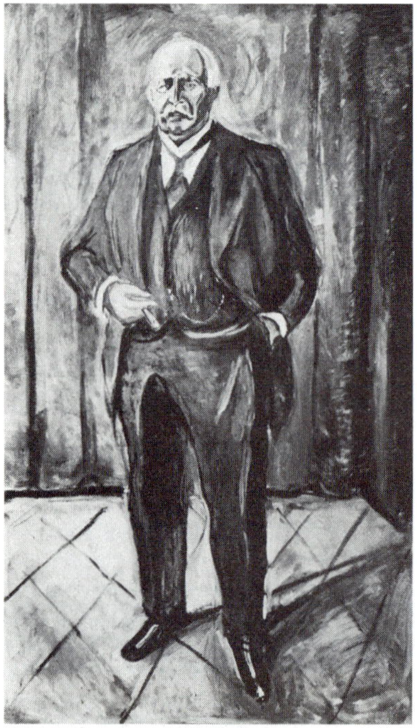

Prime Minister Otto Blehr, 1927 Oil on canvas

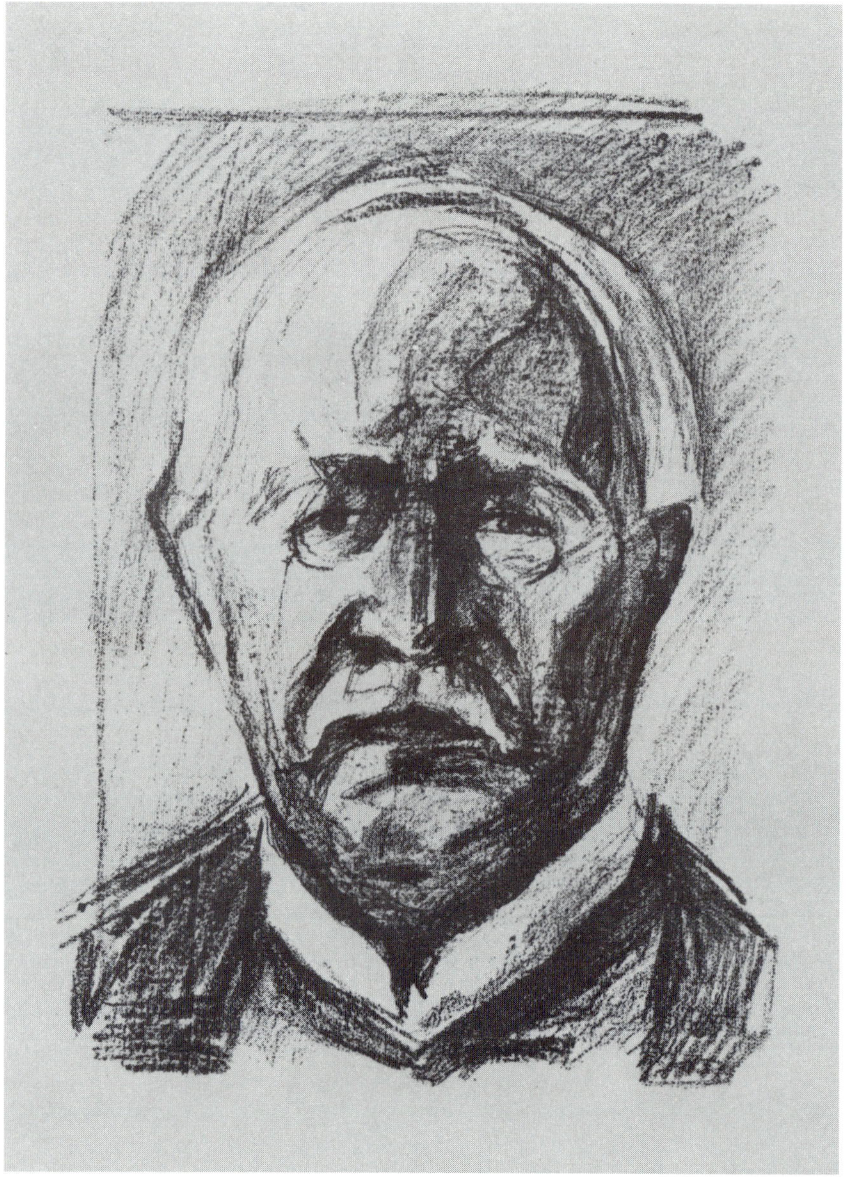

Prime Minister Otto Blehr, 1926-27 Lithograph

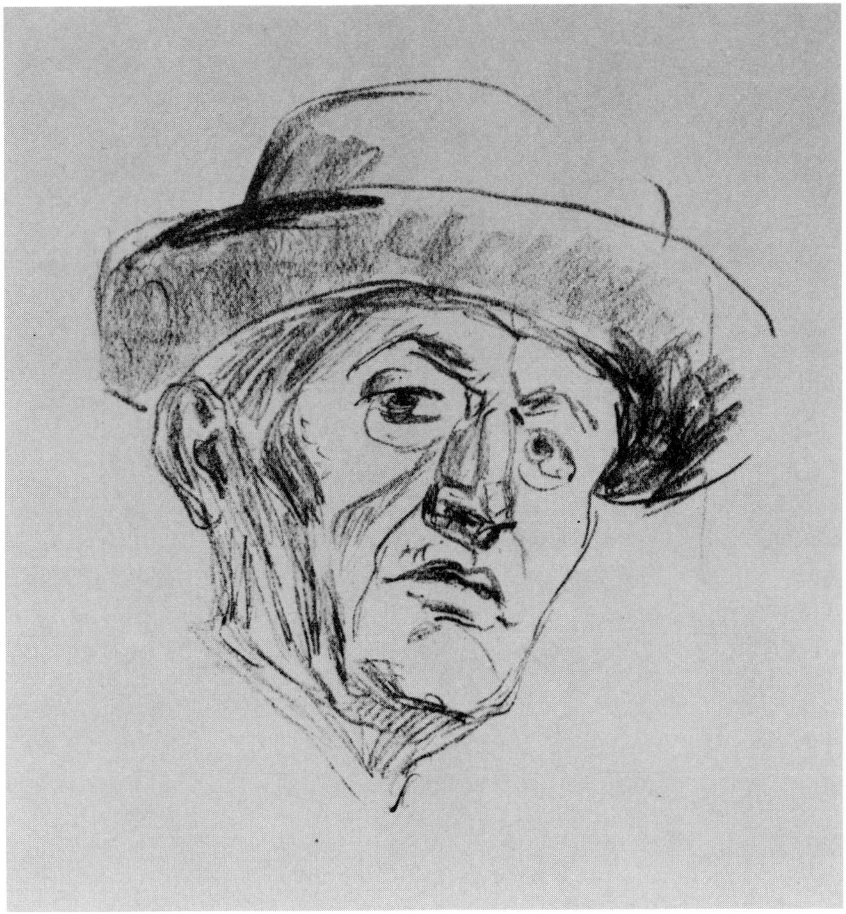

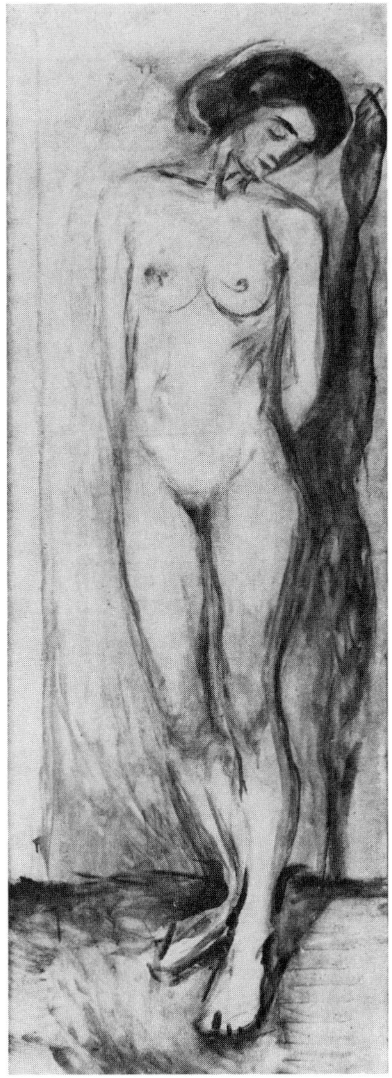

Krotkaja, 1927 Oil on canvas

Self-Portrait with Hat, 1927
Lithograph

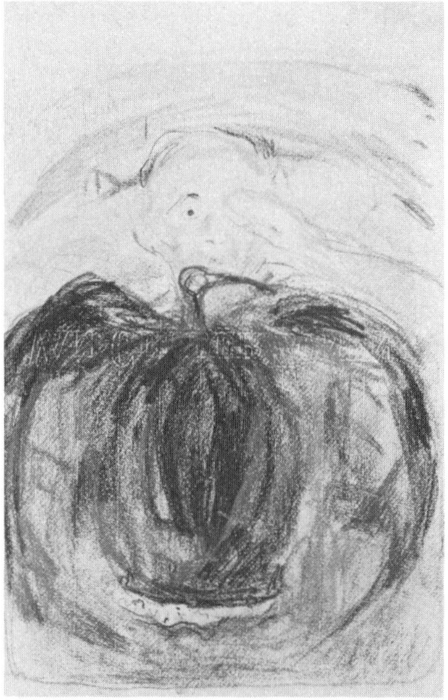

The Artist Naked and Threatening form with Bird's Head, 1930 Coloured crayon

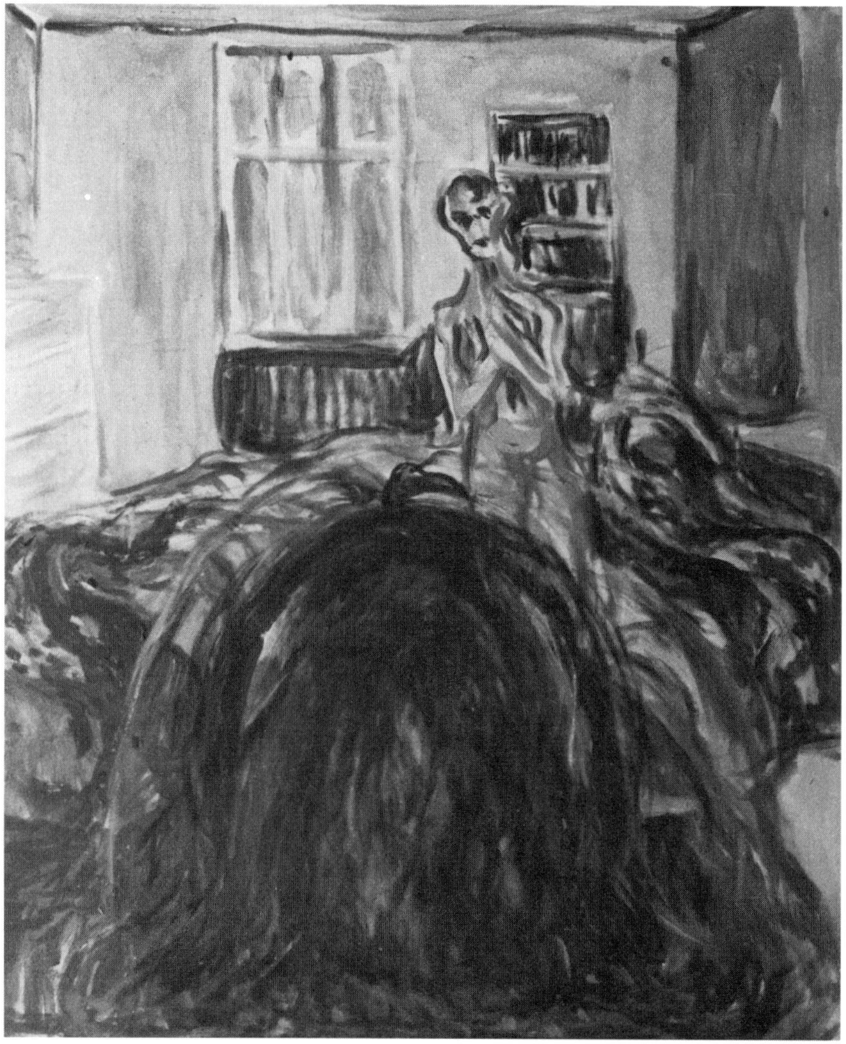

The Artist Naked and Threatening form with Bird's Head, 1930 Oil on canvas

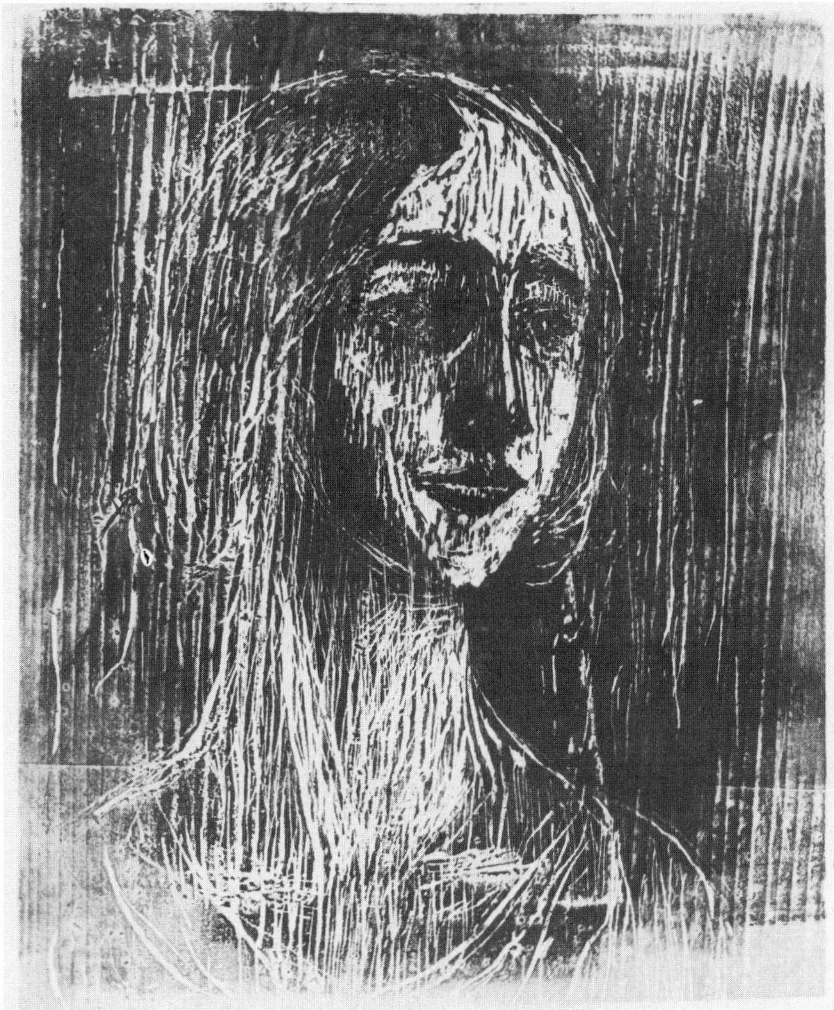

Birgitte III, 1930 Colour woodcut

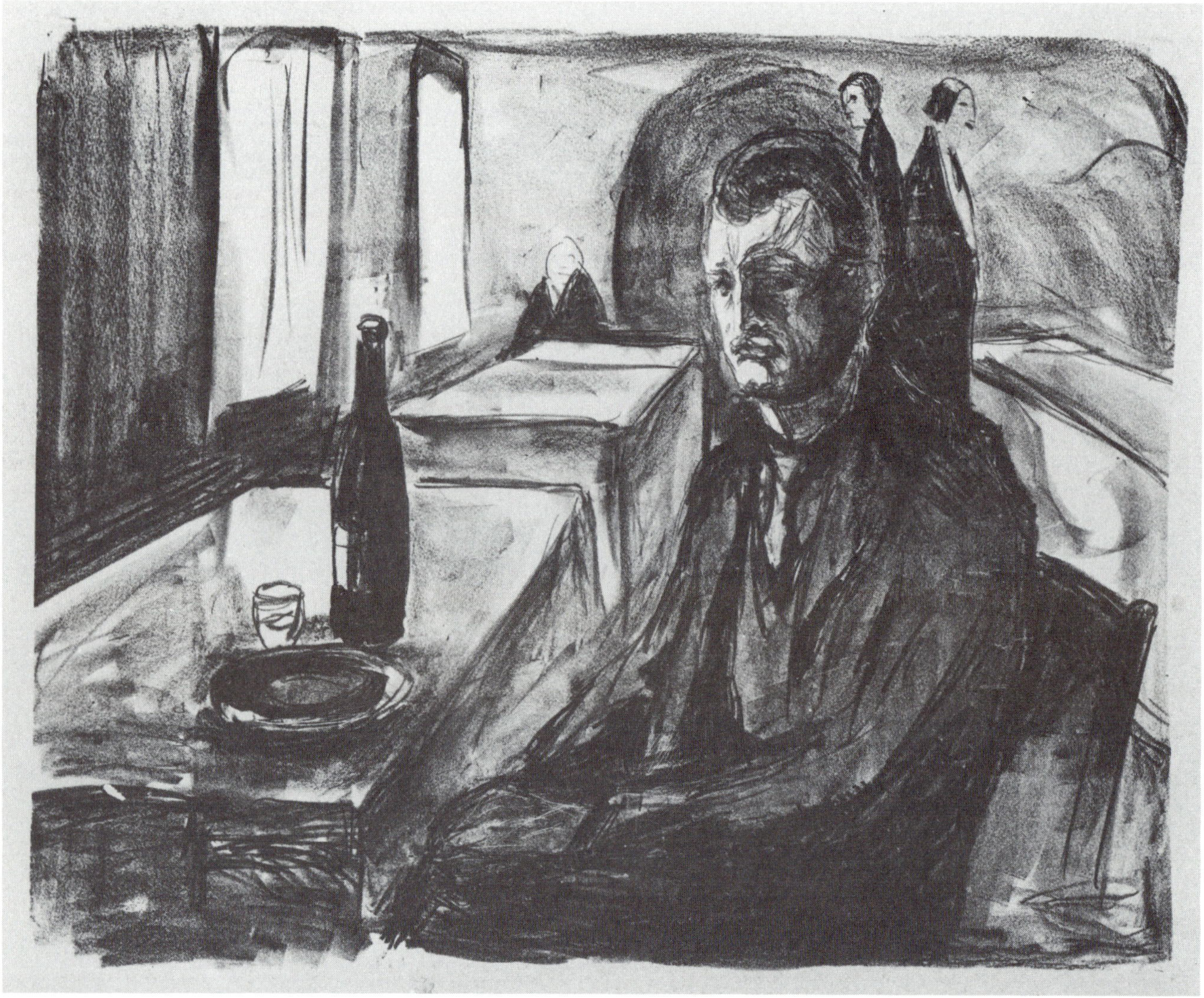

Self-portrait with Bottle of Wine,
c1930 Lithograph

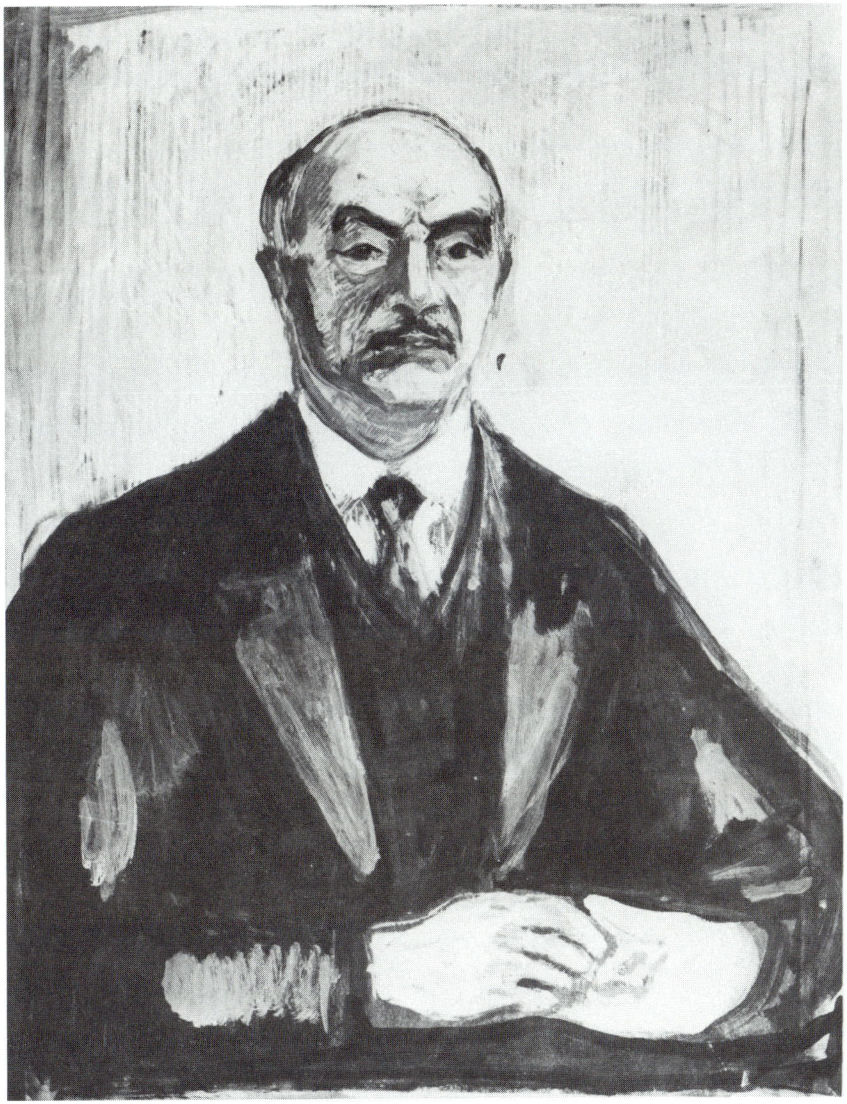

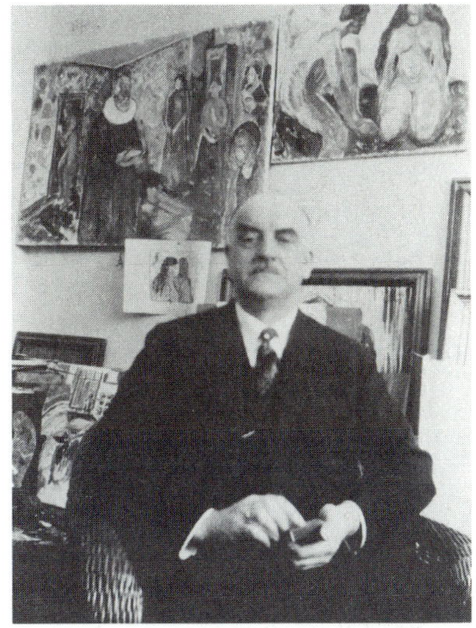

Fritz Frölich at Ekely, 1931-32

The Factory Owner Fritz Frölich, 1930-31 Woodcut and oil on board

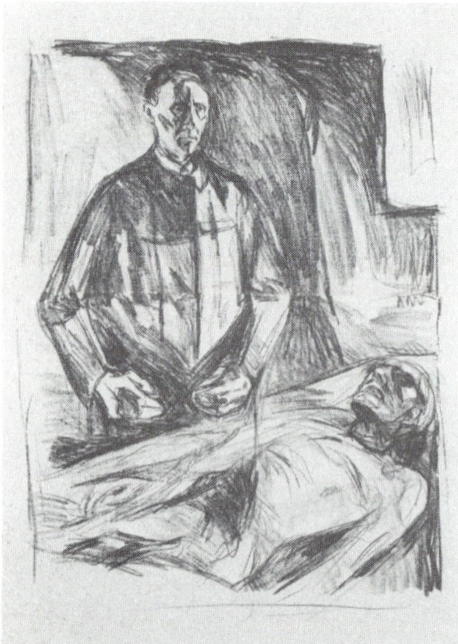

Professor Kristian Schreiner as Anatomist, 1932 Lithograph

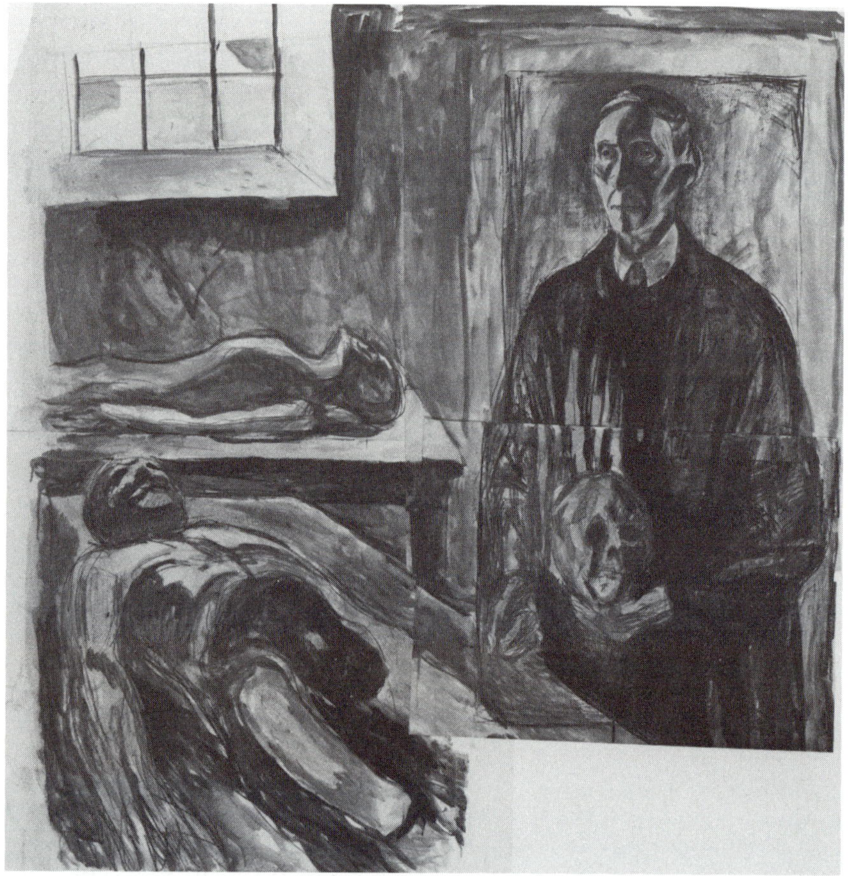

Professor Kristian Schreiner as Anatomist, 1932 Collage of two lithographs overworked with gouache

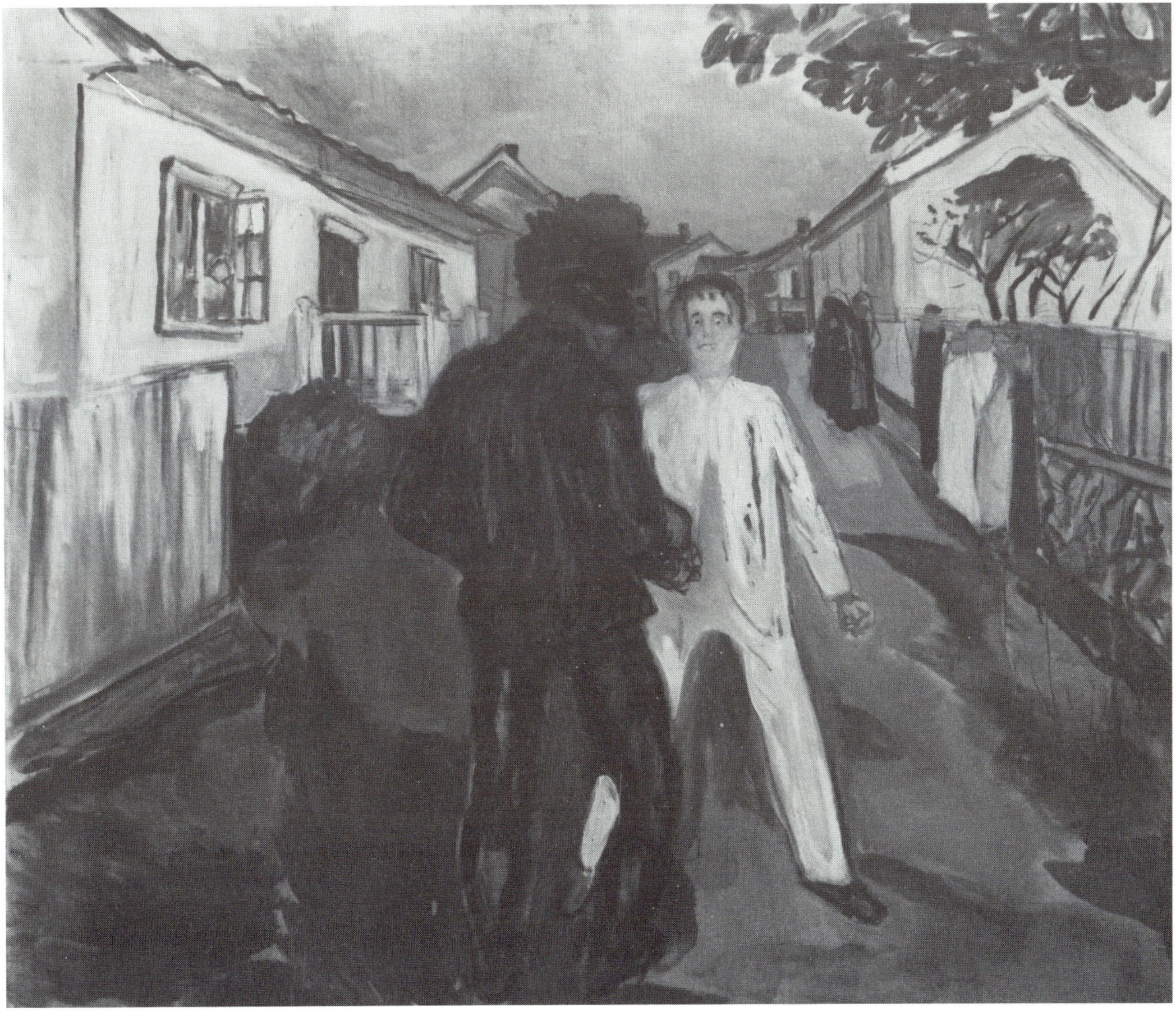

Mephistopheles II: The Fight,
1932-33 Oil on canvas

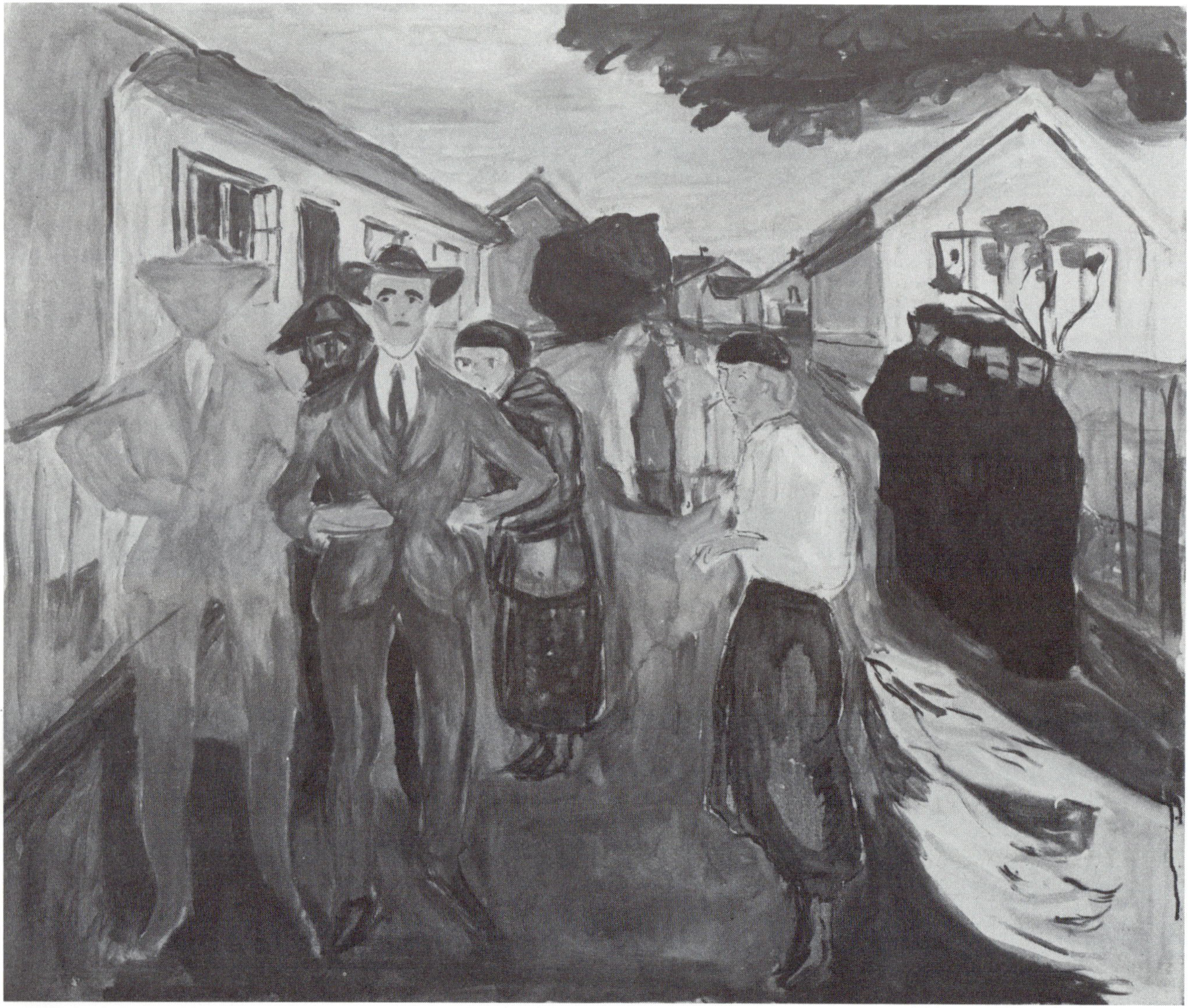

Mephistopheles I: Split Personality,
1932-35 Oil on canvas

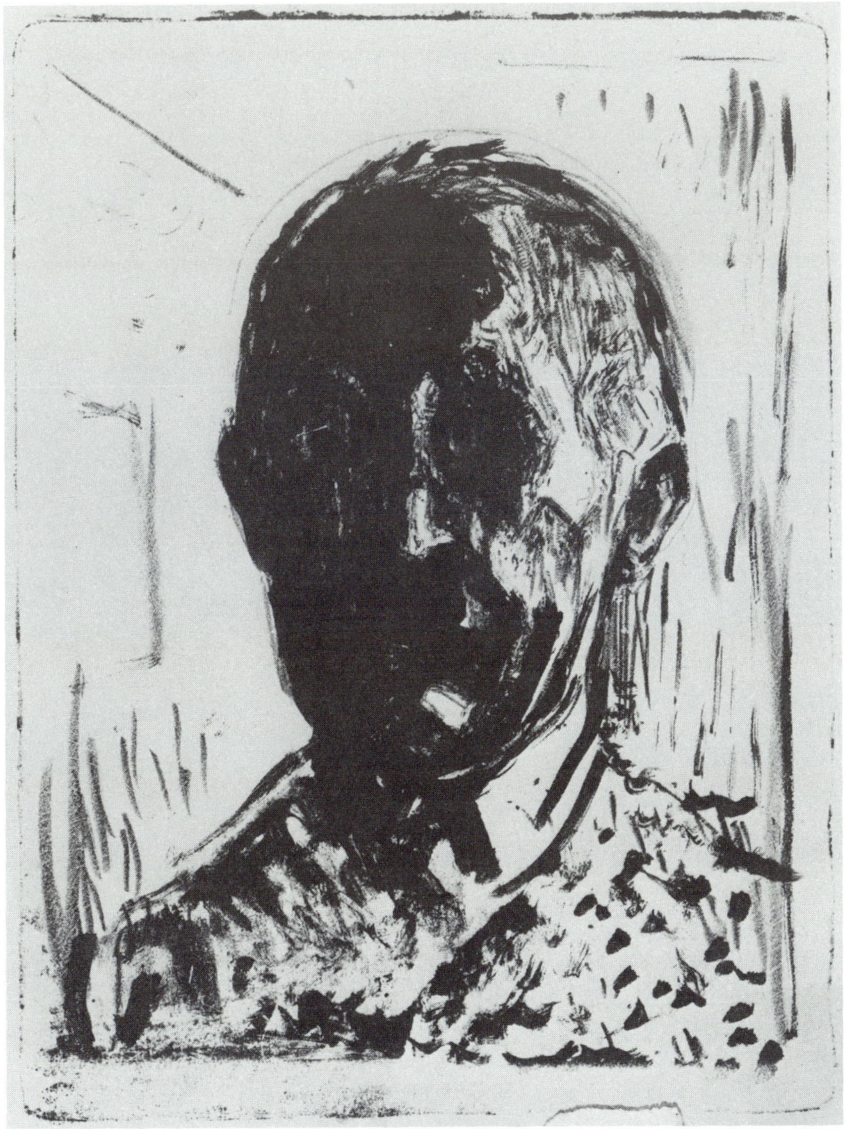

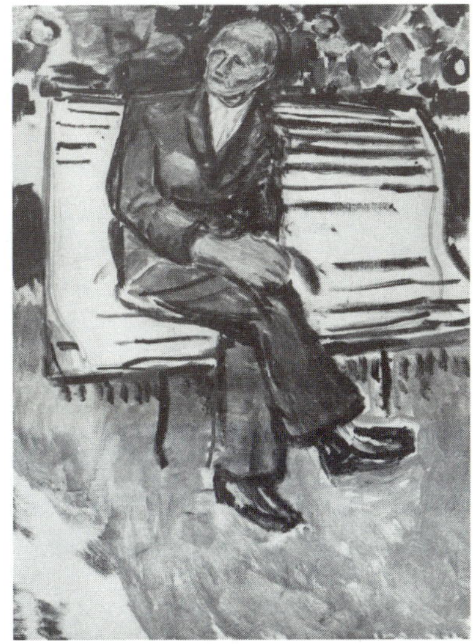

Portrait of Rolf Hansen, 1943-44
Oil on canvas

Self-Portrait, 1930-35 Lithograph

Munch in his studio in Lutzowstrasse 82, Berlin 1902

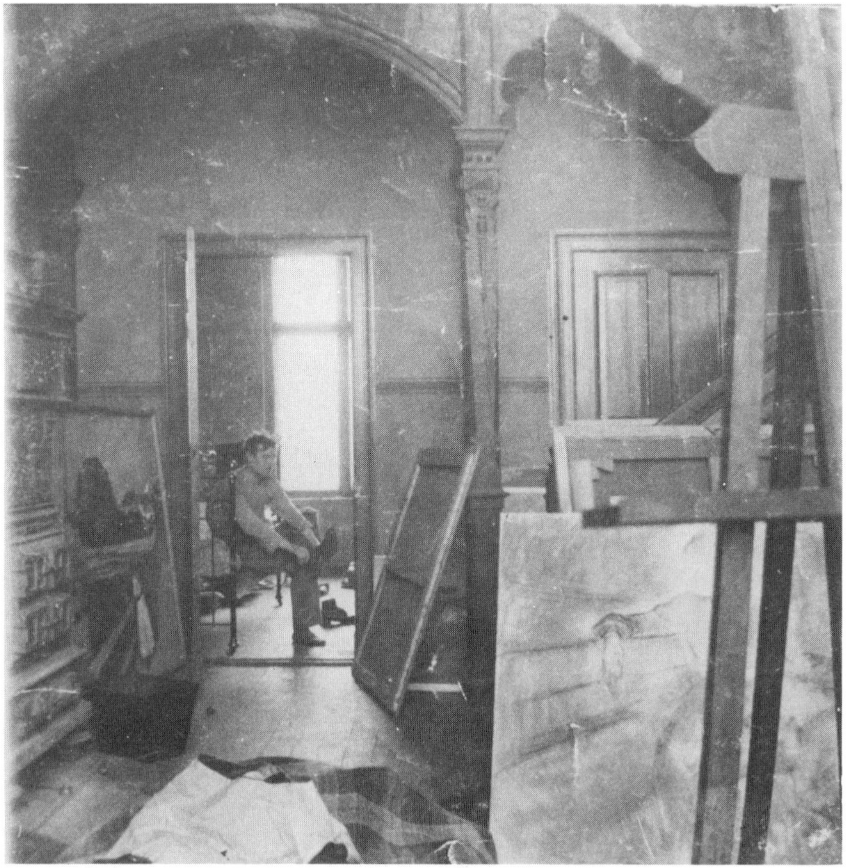

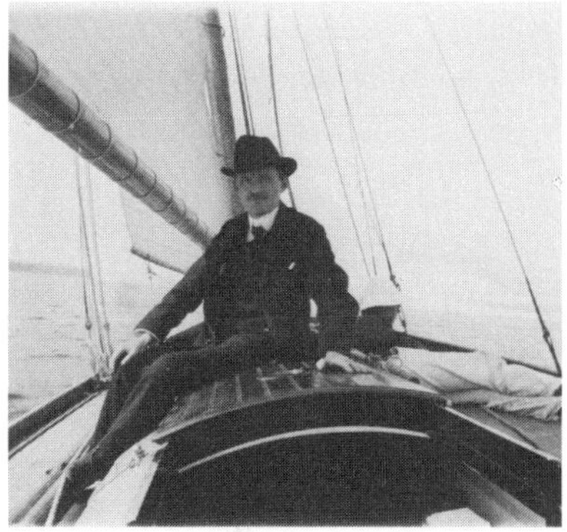

Munch sailing at Åsgårdstrand, 1903

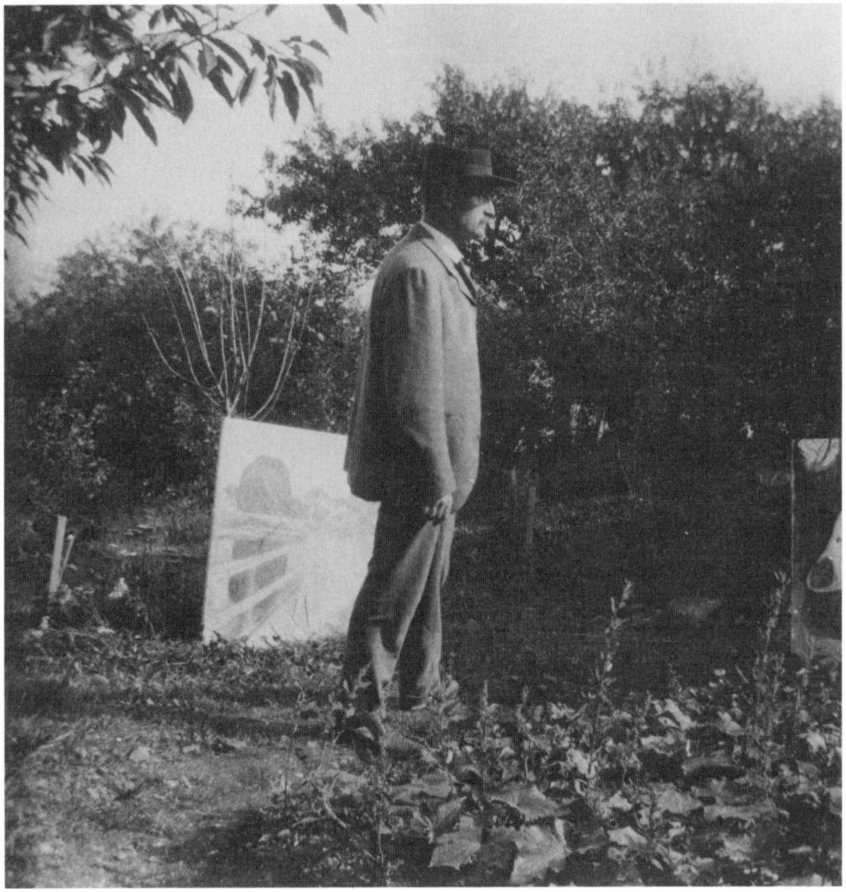

Munch in the garden at Åsgårdstrand, 1903

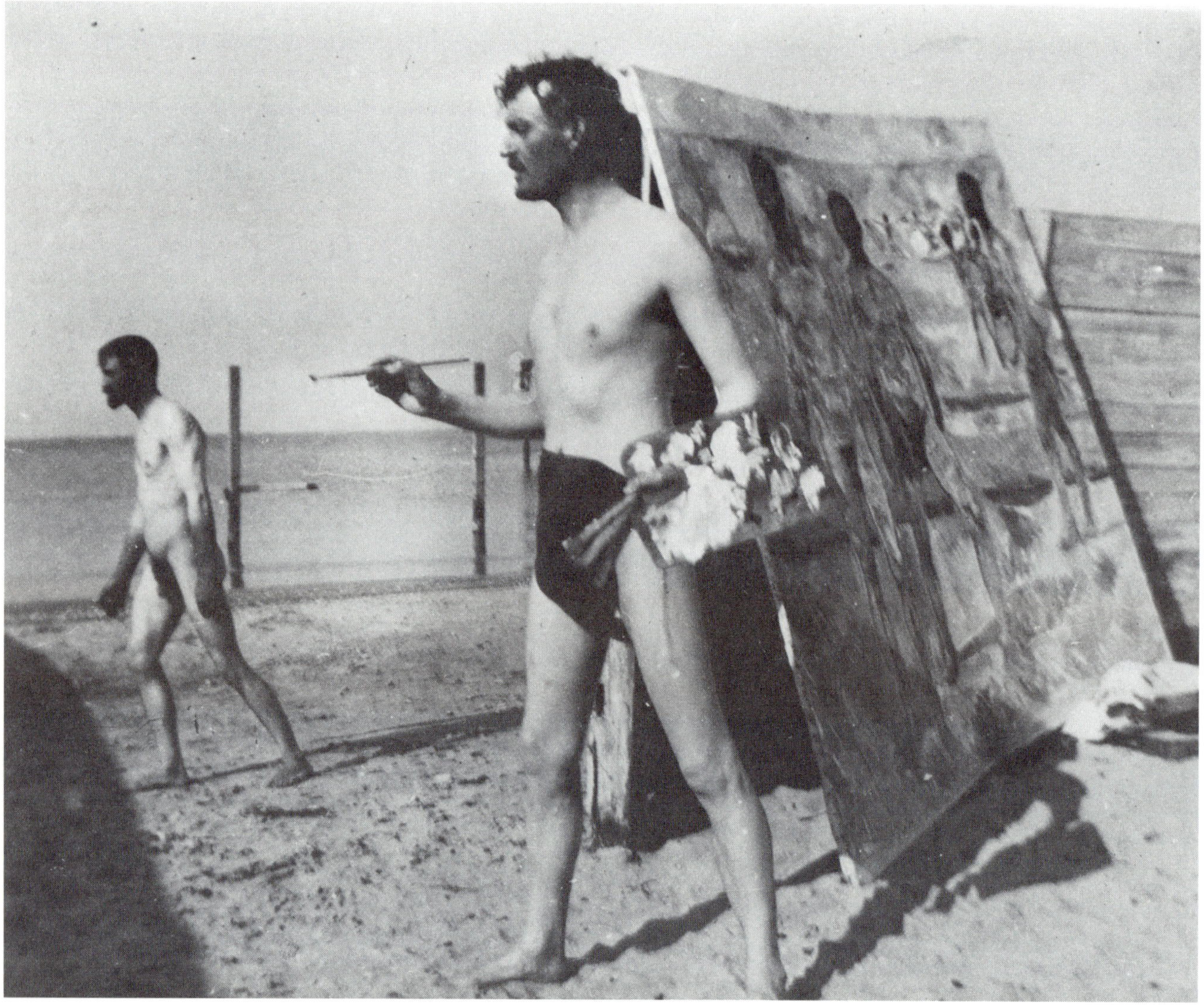

Munch painting on the beach,
Warnemünde, 1907

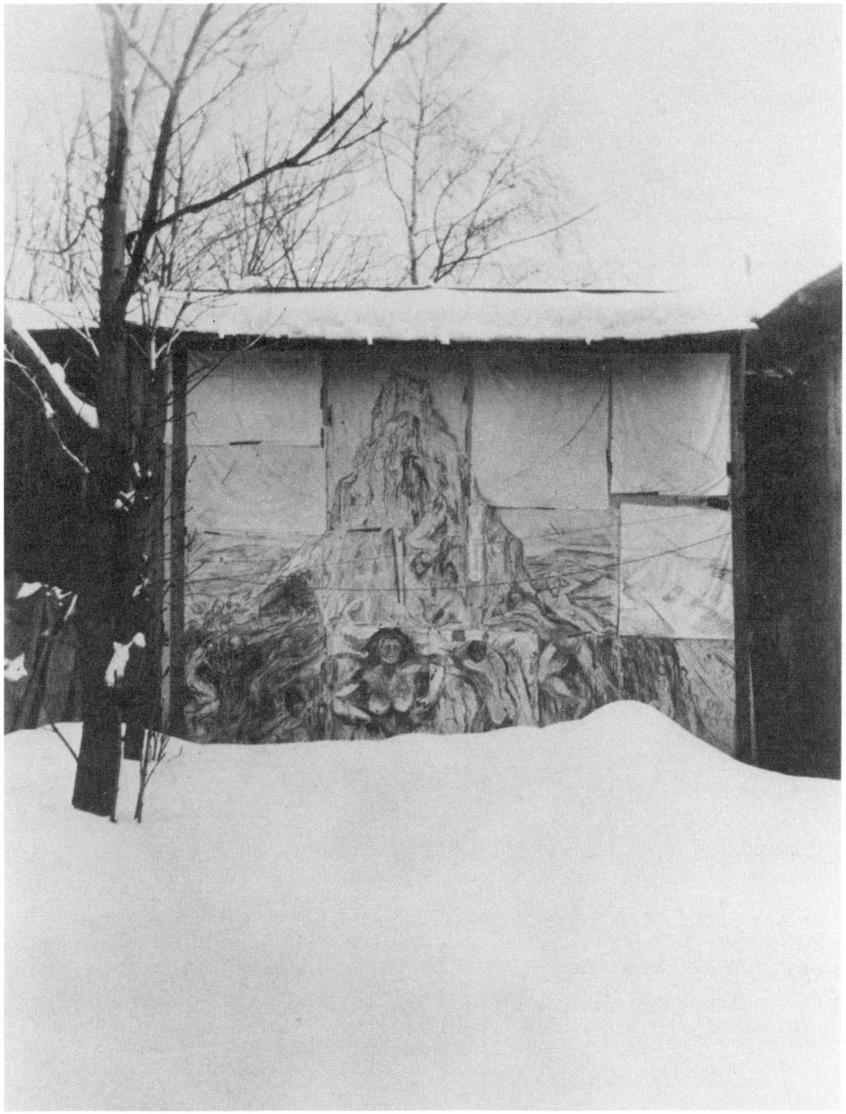

'Mountain of Mankind' outdoor studio, Ekely 1927

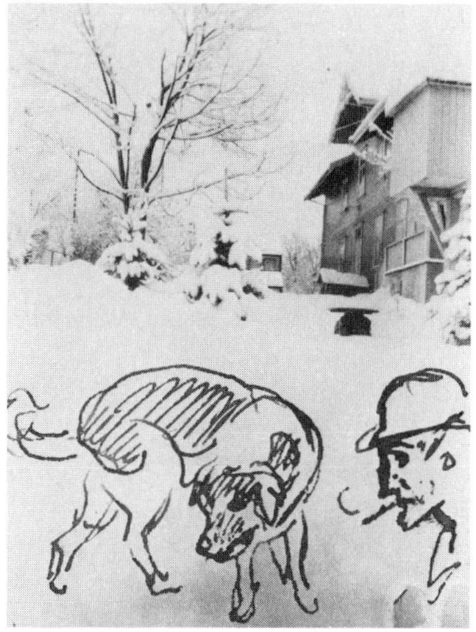

The main building in snow, Ekely, 1927 Postcard with drawing

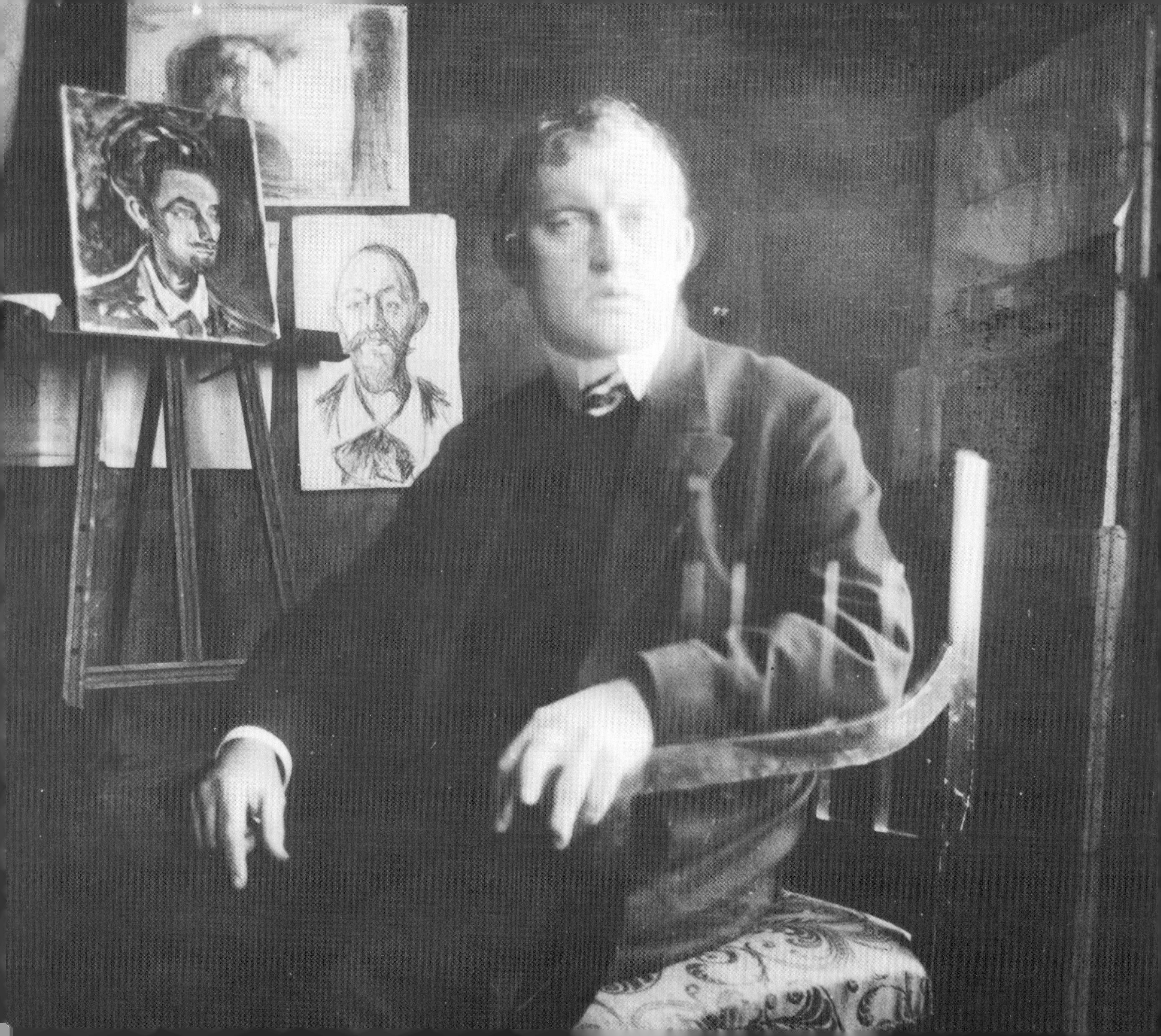

List of works

1. Self-Portrait with Skeleton Arm 1895
Lithograph 460 x 322mm
OKK G/L 192-15 Schiefler. 31

2. Tingel-Tangel 1895
(Academy of Music, Berlin)
Lithograph 410 x 630mm
OKK G/L 198-1 Schiefler. 37

3. August Strindberg 1896
Lithograph 605 x 460mm
OKK G/L 219-2 Schiefler. 77

4. August Strindberg 1896
Lithograph 605 x 460mm
OKK G/L 219-5 Schiefler. 77

5. Marcel Réja 1896
Woodcut 390 x 326mm
OKK G/L 691-7

6. Stéphane Mallarmé 1896
Lithograph 400 x 296mm
OKK G/L 221-18 Schiefler. 79

7. Self-Portrait with Lyre 1897 Indian ink, watercolour and gouache 685 x 525mm
OKK T 2460

8. Ibsen with Lighthouse 1897 (Programme poster for Ibsen's *'John Gabriel Borkman'*, Théâtre de l'Oeuvre, Paris)
Lithograph 320 x 208mm
OKK G/L 721-2

9. In Man's Brain 1897
Colour woodcut 373 x 567mm
OKK G/L 573-15 Schiefler.98

10. Man's Head in Woman's Hair 1897 Lithograph, hand-coloured 380 x 444mm
OKK G/L 544-2

11. The Kiss 1897-98
Colour woodcut 456 x 380mm
OKK G/L 578-4 Schiefler. 102B

12. The Kiss 1897-98
Colour woodcut 593 x 460mm
OKK G/L 577-7 Schiefler. 102A

13. The Kiss 1897-98
Woodcut, hand coloured
590 x 457mm
OKK G/L 577-6 Schiefler. 102A

14. Two Women on the Beach 1898
Colour woodcut 455 x 508mm
OKK G/T 589-13 Schiefler. 117

15. Henrik Ibsen at the Grand Cafe 1902
Lithograph 420 x 590mm
OKK G/L 244-6 Schiefler. 171

16. Anna and Walter Leistikow 1902
Lithograph 522 x 868mm
OKK G/L 243-9 Schiefler. 170

17. The Sin 1902
Colour lithograph 700 x 405mm
OKK G/L 241-3 Schiefler. 142

18. Standing Nude 1902
Oil on canvas 120 x 50cm
OKK M 469

19. Aase Nørregaard 1902
Oil on canvas 195.5 x 105cm
OKK M 709

20. The Operation 1902
Oil on canvas 109 x 149cm
OKK M 22

21. The Brooch: Eva Mudocci
1903 Lithograph 600 x 460mm
OKK G/L 255 Schiefler. 212

22. The Violin Concert 1903
Lithograph 480 x 560mm
OKK G/L 254-4 Schiefler. 211

23. Ingse Vibe 1903
Oil on canvas 160 x 70cm
OKK M 272

24. Self-Portrait in Hell 1903
Oil on canvas 81.5 x 65.5cm
OKK M 591

25. Self-Portrait with Brushes 1904
Oil on canvas 197 x 91cm
OKK M 751

26. Self-Portrait 1904
Oil on board 64 x 65cm
OKK M 249

27. Dance on the Shore (Linde Frieze) 1904
Oil on canvas 90 x 316cm
OKK M 719

28. Double-Portrait of the Painter Henrik Lund and His Wife Gunbjør 1905
Oil on canvas 67 x 57cm
OKK M 617

29. Sketch for Stage Set, 'Ghosts' 1906
Tempera on canvas 60 x 102cm
OKK M 984

30. Sketch for Stage Set, 'Hedda Gabler' 1906
Pencil, colour crayon and watercolour 240 x 312mm
OKK T 1581

31. Sketch for Stage Set, 'Hedda Gabler' 1906
Indian ink and gouache on board 342 x 497mm
OKK T 1583

32. Friedrich Nietzsche
1906-07 Coloured crayon and charcoal on paper 200 x 130cm
OKK T 2555

33. Study for Portrait of Friedrich Nietzsche 1906-07
Coloured crayon and charcoal on board 73 x 101cm
OKK T 254

34. Children in the Street, Warnemünde 1907
Oil on canvas 99 x 79cm
OKK M 578

35. Elizabeth Förster-Nietzsche 1907 Oil on canvas 164 x 100cm OKK M 378

36. Weeping Girl 1907
Oil on canvas 109 x 149cm
OKK M 689

37. Olga and Rosa Meissner
1907 Oil on canvas 70 x 80cm
OKK M 106

38. Desire 1907
Oil on canvas 85 x 130cm
OKK M 552

39. Helge Rode 1908
Oil on canvas 48 x 40cm
OKK M 111

40. Self-Portrait with Cigarette 1908-09
Lithograph 566 x455mm
OKK G/L 277 Schiefler. 282

41. Dr Daniel Jacobson
1908-09 Lithograph 515 x 297mm
OKK G/L 269-6 Schiefler. 273

42. Dr Daniel Jacobson 1909
Oil on canvas 204 x 111.5cm
OKK M 359 A

43. Dr Daniel Jacobson 1909
Oil on canvas 55 x 43cm
OKK M 230

44. John Gabriel Borkman. Last Scene 1909-10
Charcoal 480 x 650mm
OKK T 2116

45. Workers in the Snow
1910 Bronze sculpture
70 x 56.5 x45cm
OKK S 1

46. Weeping Girl 1909-14
Bronze sculpture
38.2 x 27.5 x 29.4cm
OKK S 2

47. The Sacrament 1915
Oil on canvas 120 x 180cm
OKK M 416

48. The Son 1920
Woodcut 490 x 600mm
OKK G/T 651-1 Sch. 492

49. Osvald 1920
(From Ibsen's Play *'Ghosts'*)
Lithograph, hand-coloured
390 x 500mm
OKK G/L 421-1 Sch. 487

50. Birgit Prestøe 1925
Oil on canvas 90 x 100cm
OKK M 744

51. Prime Minister Otto Blehr
1926-27 Lithograph 355 x255mm
OKK G/L 489-7

52. Prime Minister Otto Blehr
1927 Oil on canvas 190 x 110cm
OKK M 701

53. Self-Portrait with Hat
1927 Lithograph 202 x 191mm
OKK G/L 456-26

54. Krotkaja 1927
Oil on canvas 177 x 58cm
OKK M 752

55. Study of Munch's Injured Retina 1930
Watercolour 500 x 646mm
OKK T 2166

56. The Artist Naked and Threatening Form with Bird's Head 1930
Oil on canvas 80 x 64cm
OKK M 334

57. The Artist Naked and Threatening Form with Bird's Head 1930
Oil on canvas 80 x 64cm
OKK M 341

58. The Artist Naked and Threatening Form with Bird's Head 1930
Coloured crayon 502 x 315mm
OKK T 2152

59. Birgitte II 1930
Woodcut 388 x 313mm
OKK G/T 702-4

60. Birgitte III 1930
Colour woodcut 600 x 343mm
OKK G/T 703-8

61. Weeping Girl 1930
Lithograph, hand-coloured
400 x 388mm
OKK G/L 540-6

62. Self-Portrait with Bottle of Wine c.1930
Lithograph 420 x 515mm
OKK G/L 492-4

63. The Factory Owner Fritz Frölich 1930-31
Woodcut and oil on board
89 x 66cm
OKK M 471

64. Self-Portrait 1930-35
Lithograph 450 x 332mm
OKK G/L 488-2

65. Professor Kristian Schreiner as Anatomist 1932
Lithograph 763 x 555mm
OKK G/L 551-1

66. Professor Kristian Schreiner as Anatomist 1932
Collage of two lithographs
overworked with gouache
137.5 x 135,5cm
OKK G/L 553-1, 552-6, T566, 565

67. Mephistopheles II : The Fight 1932-33
Oil on canvas 105 x 120cm
OKK M 554

68. Mephistopheles I : Split Personality 1932-35
Oil on canvas 100 x 117cm
OKK M 553

69. Self-Portrait Between Clock and Bed 1940-42
Oil on canvas 149.5 x 120.5cm
OKK M 23

70. Self-Portrait at 2.15am
1940-44
Gouache 515 x 645mm
OKK T 2433

71. Portrait of Rolf Hansen
1943-44
Oil on canvas 109 x 80mm
OKK M 565

Photographs taken by Edvard Munch

1. Edvard Munch sitting on a trunk in his studio in Lützowstrasse 82, Berlin
1902
Original photograph, Self-Portrait
OKK B 2147 (F)

2. Edvard Munch sitting on a trunk in his studio in Lützowstrasse 82, Berlin
1902
Original photograph, Self-Portrait
OKK B 2148 (F)

3. Edvard Munch on the bedside in his studio in Lutzowstrasse 82, Berlin
1902
Original Photograph, Self-Portrait
OKK B 2149 (F)

4. Model posing in Munch's studio, Lutzowstrasse 82, Berlin 1902
Original photograph
Photograph by Edvard Munch
OKK B 2927 (F)

5. Model posing in Munch's studio, Lützowstrasse 82, Berlin 1902
Original photograph
Photograph by Edvard Munch
OKK B 2184 (F)

6. Marta Sandal in Munch's studio, Lützowstrasse 82, Berlin 1902
Original photograph
Photograph by Edvard Munch
OKK B 2159 (F)

7. The brothers Wieck in Munch's studio, Lützowstrasse 82, Berlin
1902
Original photograph
Photograph by Edvard Munch
OKK B 2145 (F)

8. Walter Leistikow in his studio, Berlin 1902
Original photograph
Photograph by Edvard Munch
OKK B 2883 (F)

9. Edvard Munch in front of gravestones in Berlin 1902
Original photograph
Photograph taken by Albert Kollmann
OKK B 2843 (F)

10. Albert Kollmann in front of gravestones in Berlin 1902
Original photograph
Photograph by Edvard Munch
OKK B 2844 (F)

11. Edvard Munch's exhibition at Blomqvist, Kristiania 1902
Original photograph
Photograph by Edvard Munch
OKK B 2143 (F)

12. Edvard Munch's exhibition at Blomqvist, Kristiania 1902
Original photograph
Photograph by Edvard Munch
OKK B 2144 (F)

13. Edvard Munch in bed
probably 1902
Original photograph, Self-portrait
OKK B 2836 (F)

14. Edvard Munch's childhood home, Pilestredet 30b, Kristiania probably 1902
Original photograph
Photograph by Edvard Munch
OKK B 2977 (F)

15. From the backyard in Pilestredet 30b, Kristiania
probably 1902
Original photograph
Photograph by Edvard Munch
OKK B 2665 (F)

16. The backyard in Pilestredet 30b, Kristiania
probably 1902
Original photograph
Photograph by Edvard Munch
OKK B 2976 (F)

17. The entrance to Pilestredet 30b, Kristiania
probably 1902
Original photograph
Photograph by Edvard Munch
OKK B 2845 (F)

18. Edvard Munch's aunt Karen and sister Inger in front of Olaf Ryes plass 2 and 4, Kristiania probably 1902
Original photograph
Photograph by Edvard Munch
OKK B 2664 (F)

19. 'The Operation' in the home of Dr Linde, Lübeck
1902
Original photograph
Photograph by Edvard Munch
OKK B 2146 (F)

20. The exhibition premises of Paul Cassirer, Berlin 1903
Original photograph
Photograph by Edvard Munch
OKK B 2893 (F)

21. Edvard Munch sailing at Åsgårdstrand 1903
Original photograph
Photograph by Edvard Munch
OKK B 2736 (F)

22. Edvard Munch in the garden of his house at Åsgårdstrand 1903
Original photograph
Photograph by Edvard Munch
OKK B 2181 (F)

23. Edvard Munch posing in the nude, Åsgårdstrand 1903
Original photograph
Photograph by Edvard Munch
OKK B 3223 (F)

24. Ingse Vibe and friends, Åsgårdstrand 1903
Original photograph
Photograph by Edvard Munch
OKK B 3086 (F)

25. Edvard Munch posing, Åsgårdstrand 1904
Original photograph
Photograph by Edvard Munch
OKK B 2835 (F)

26. Edvard Munch in his working shirt, Åsgårdstrand
1904
Original photograph
Photograph by Edvard Munch
OKK B 2834 (F)

27. Edvard Munch with L Ravensberg and an unidentified person in front of 'Bathing Boys', Åsgårdstrand 1904
Original photograph
Photograph by Edvard Munch
OKK B 2833 (F)

28. Ludvig Ravensberg, Åsgårdstrand 1904
Original photograph
Photograph by Edvard Munch
OKK B 2705 (F), a

29. 'Bathing Boys' in the garden, Åsgårdstrand 1904
Original photograph
Photograph by Edvard Munch
OKK B 2705 (F), b

30. Edvard Munch inside his house at Åsgårdstrand
probably 1904
Original photograph, Self-portrait
OKK B 1859 (F)

31. Edvard Munch with an unidentified young girl, Åsgårdstrand 1904
Original photograph
Photograph by Edvard Munch
OKK B 1861 (F)

32. Paintings from the 'Linde Frieze' in the garden at Åsgårdstrand 1904
Original photograph
Photograph by Edvard Munch
OKK B 1860 (F)

33. Edvard Munch in an unidentified room on the Continent probably 1906
Original photograph, Self-portrait
OKK B 2385 (F)

34. Edvard Munch in an unidentified room on the Continent probably 1906
Original photograph
Photograph by Edvard Munch
OKK B 2385 (F), mirror-version

35. Edvard Munch in an unidentified room probably 1906
Original photograph, Self-portrait
OKK B 2491 (F)

36. Edvard Munch in an unidentified room probably 1906
Self-portrait
OKK B 2841 (F)

37. From Munch's exhibition at Paul Cassirer, Berlin 1907
Original photograph
Photograph by Edvard Munch
OKK B 1831 (F), b

38. From Edvard Munch's exhibition at Paul Cassirer, Berlin 1907
Copy from original negative
Photograph by Edvard Munch
OKK B 1831 (F), c

39. Edvard Munch in the hall of Am Strom 53, Warnemünde 1907
Copy from original negative
Self-portrait
OKK B 1863 (F)

40. Am Strom 53, Warnemünde 1907
Original photograph
Photograph by Edvard Munch
OKK B 2831 (F)

41. Edvard Munch on the veranda, Am Strom 53, Warnemünde 1907
Self-portrait
OKK B 2645 (F)

42. Male Model on the beach, Warnemünde 1907
Original photograph
Photograph by Edvard Munch
OKK B 1295 (F), b

43. Edvard Munch posing on the beach, Warnemünde
1907
Original Photograph
Self-portrait
OKK B 2827 (F)

44. Edvard Munch posing on the beach, Warnemünde
1907
Original photograph, Self-portrait
OKK B 2472 (F)

45. Edvard Munch on the beach, Warnemünde 1907
Original photograph, Self-portrait
OKK B 2828 (F)

46. Edvard Munch painting on the beach, Warnemünde
1907
Original photograph, Self-portrait
OKK B 1295 (F)

47. Edvard Munch and Rosa Meissner on the beach, Warnemünde 1907
Original photograph
Photograph by Edvard Munch
Mirror version of no 48
OKK B 2822 (F)

48. Edvard Munch and Rosa Meissner on the beach, Warnemünde 1907
Original photograph
Photograph by Edvard Munch
OKK B 2825 (F)

49. Edvard Munch and Rosa Meissner on the beach, Warnemünde 1907
Original photograph
Photograph by Edvard Munch
OKK B 2821 (F)

50. Rosa and Olga Meissner on the beach, Warnemünde
1907
Original photograph
Photograph by Edvard Munch
OKK B 2826 (F)

51. Edvard Munch's housekeeper at Am Strom 53, Warnemünde 1907
Original photograph
Photograph by Edvard Munch
OKK B 2838 (F)

52. Edvard Munch and his housekeeper at Am Strom 53, Warnemünde 1907
Original photograph, Self-portrait
OKK B 2837 (F)

53. Rosa Meissner at the Hotel Rohne, Warnemünde 1907
Original photograph
Photograph by Edvard Munch
OKK B 1099 (F)

54. Edvard Munch at Dr Jacobson's clinic, Copenhagen 1908-09
Original photograph, Self-portrait
OKK B 2848 (F)

55. Edvard Munch at the breakfast table at Dr Jacobson's clinic, Copenhagen 1908-09
Copy from original negative
Self-portrait
OKK B 1355 (F)

56. Edvard Munch 'a la Marat' by the bath tub at Dr Jacobson's clinic, Copenhagen 1908-09
Copy from original photograph
Self-portrait
OKK B 1855

57. Two nurses at Dr Jacobson's clinic, Copenhagen 1908-09
Copy from original negative
Photograph by Edvard Munch
OKK B 1858 (F)

58. Nurse in dark at Dr Jacobson's clinic, Copenhagen 1908-09
Copy from original negative
Photograph by Edvard Munch
OKK B 1356 (F)

59. Nurse in corridor of Dr Jacobson's clinic, Copenhagen 1908-09
Original photograph
Photograph by Edvard Munch
OKK B 2840 (F)

60. Nurse in white at Dr Jacobson's clinic, Copenhagen 1908-09
Original photograph
Photograph by Edvard Munch
OKK B 2790 (F)

61. Edvard Munch in his room at Dr Jacobson's clinic, Copenhagen 1908-09
Original photograph, Self-portrait
OKK B1857 (F)

62. Ludvig Ravensberg and his portrait, Kragerø 1909-10
Original photograph
Photograph by Edvard Munch
OKK B 2706 (F)

63. Edvard Munch between portraits of Ludvig Ravensberg and Jappe Nilssen, Kragerø 1909-10
Original photograph
Photograph by L Ravensberg
OKK B 2842 (F)

64. Christian Gierlöff, Kragerø 1909-10
Copy from original negative
Photograph by Edvard Munch
OKK B 2926 (F)

65. Edvard Munch in his studio at 'Skrubben', Kragerø 1909-10
Copy from original negative
Self-portrait
OKK B 1864 (F)

66. Edvard Munch in his studio at 'Skrubben', Kragerø 1909-10
Copy from original negative
Self-portrait
OKK B 1866 (F)

67. Edvard Munch with sculpture study for a national monument, Kragerø 1910
Copy from original photograph
Photograph by Edvard Munch
OKK B 2349 (F)

68. The harbour, Kragerø probably 1910
Original photograph
Photograph by Edvard Munch
OKK B 1898 (F)

69. The harbour, Kragerø probably 1910
Original photograph
Photograph by Edvard Munch
OKK B 2900 (F)

70. Thorvald Stang at 'Skrubben', Kragerø 1909-10
Original photograph
Photograph by Edvard Munch
OKK B 2901 (F)

71. The portait of Rolf Stenersen at Ekely 1927
Original photographs
Photograph by Edvard Munch
OKK B 3229 (F)

72. 'Street in Kragerø' on an easel, Ekely 1927
Original photograph
Photograph by Edvard Munch
OKK B 3232 (F)

73. 'The Murderess' (1907) on an easel, Ekely 1927
Original photograph
Photograph by Edvard Munch
OKK B 3235 (F)

74. 'Kneeling Model' on an easel, Ekely 1927
Original photograph
Photograph by Edvard Munch
OKK B 3233 (F)

75. The gardener's house in snow, Ekely 1927
Postcard
Photography by Edvard Munch
OKK B 3004 (F)

76. The main building in snow, Ekely 1927
Postcard with drawing
Photograph by Edvard Munch
OKK B 3005 (F)

77. The veranda at Ekely 1927
Copy of original negative
Photograph by Edvard Munch
OKK B 2953 (F)

78. The outdoor studio in snow, Ekely 1927
Original photograph
Photograph by Edvard Munch
OKK B 3240 (F)

79. 'Mountain of Mankind', outdoor studio, Ekely 1927
Original photograph
Photograph by Edvard Munch
OKK B 3238 (F)

80. Edvard Munch in profile with hat, Ekely 1930
Original photograph, Self-portrait
OKK B 2980 (F)

81. Edvard Munch in front of his winter studio, Ekely 1930
Original photograph, Self-portrait
OKK B 2910 (F)

82. Edvard Munch with hat, Ekely 1930
Original photograph, Self-portrait
OKK B 2911

83. Edvard Munch with hat, Ekely 1930
Original photograph, Self-portrait
OKK B 2881 (F)

84. Edvard Munch in front of his house, Ekely 1930
Original photograph, Self-portrait
OKK B 2882 (F)

85. Edvard Munch with glasses and hat, Ekely 1930
Original photograph, Self-portrait
OKK B 2909 (F)

86. Edvard Munch in profile with hat, Ekely 1930
Original photograph, Self-portrait
OKK B 3247 (F)

87. Edvard Munch on the veranda, Ekely 1930
Original photograph, Self-portrait
OKK B 2914 (F)

88. Edvard Munch on the veranda, Ekely 1930
Original photograph, Self-portrait
OKK B 2913 (F)

89. Edvard Munch in profile in the garden at Ekely with the winter studio in the background 1930
Original photograph, Self-portrait
OKK B 1363 (F)

90. Edvard Munch in front of 'Death of Marat' I 1930
Copy from original negative
Self-portrait
OKK B 2917 (F)

91. Edvard Munch in front of 'Death of Marat' II 1930
Original photograph, Self-portrait
OKK B 2919 (F)

92. Edvard Munch in front of 'Death of Marat' III, Ekely
1930
Original photograph, Self-portrait
OKK B 2915 (F)

93. Edvard Munch in front of 'Death of Marat' IV, Ekely
1930
Original photograph, Self-portrait
OKK B 2916 (F)

94. Edvard Munch in front of 'Youth on the Beach' (1904), Ekely 1930
Copy from original negative
Self-portrait
OKK B 3248 (F)

95. Edvard Munch in front of 'Family Tree', Ekely 1930
Original photograph
Self-portrait
OKK B 2920 (F)

96. Edvard Munch in front of 'Young Girl with Dog' I, Ekely
1930
Copy from original negative
Self-portrait
OKK B 2924 (F)

97. Edvard Munch in front of 'Young Girl with Dog' II 1930
Copy from original negative
Self-portrait
OKK B 2880 (F)

98. Edvard Munch in front of 'Metabolism', Ekely 1930
Original photograph
Self-portrait
OKK B 2641 (F)

99. 'Metabolism' and 'Red Barn' with mirror effects, Ekely 1931-32
Original photograph
Photograph by Edvard Munch
OKK B 3268 (F)

100. From the winter studio, Ekely 1931-32
Original photograph
Photograph Edvard Munch
OKK B 3277 (F)

101. Fritz Frölich at Ekely
1931-32
Original photograph
Photograph by Edvard Munch
OKK B 3250 (F)

102. The portrait of Fritz Frölich on an easel, Ekely
1931-32
Original photograph
Photograph by Edvard Munch
OKK B 3258 (F)

Published by The Polytechnic Gallery, Newcastle upon Tyne

Edited by Mara-Helen Wood, William Varley

Photographs ©Munch Museum, Oslo

Designed by Stephen & Sue Bland

Printed by Wards Group Limited

Typeset by The Setting Studio

Exhibition & Tour organised by Mara-Helen Wood, Curator,
Newcastle Polytechnic Gallery

Lenders to the Exhibition: The Munch Museum, Oslo

Tour

Hatton Gallery, Newcastle University	2 May - 10 June, 1989
and Newcastle Polytechnic Gallery	2 May - 16 June
The City Art Centre, Edinburgh	5 August - 16 September
City Art Gallery, Manchester	23 September - 5 November
The Museum of Modern Art, Oxford	14 January - 18 March, 1990